The Hellenistic Astrologer: Contributions and Contexts of Key Historical Events

Table of Contents

CHAPTER 1: INTRODUCTION TO HELLENISTIC ASTROLOGY 1

HISTORICAL OVERVIEW 1
KEY CONCEPTS IN HELLENISTIC ASTROLOGY 2

CHAPTER 2: THE DEVELOPMENT OF WHOLE SIGN HOUSES 5

ORIGINS AND EVOLUTION 5
COMPARISON WITH OTHER HOUSE SYSTEMS 6

CHAPTER 3: THE TROPICAL ZODIAC IN HELLENISTIC ASTROLOGY 9

DEFINITION AND SIGNIFICANCE 9
DIFFERENCES BETWEEN TROPICAL AND SIDEREAL ZODIAC 10

CHAPTER 4: KEY HISTORICAL FIGURES IN HELLENISTIC ASTROLOGY 13

PTOLEMY AND HIS CONTRIBUTIONS 13
VETTIUS VALENS: A PIONEERING ASTROLOGER............................ 14
OTHER INFLUENTIAL ASTROLOGERS....................................... 16

CHAPTER 5: THE INFLUENCE OF THE HELLENISTIC PERIOD ON
ASTROLOGY PRACTICES 18

CULTURAL EXCHANGES AND THEIR IMPACT 18
THE INTEGRATION OF ASTRONOMY AND ASTROLOGY........................ 19

CHAPTER 6: ASTROLOGY AND POLITICAL DECISIONS IN ANCIENT
GREECE...22

THE ROLE OF ASTROLOGY IN STATECRAFT 22

CHAPTER 7: THE IMPACT OF HELLENISTIC ASTROLOGY ON ROMAN
PRACTICES...26

ADOPTION AND ADAPTATION IN ROMAN SOCIETY........................... 26
KEY ROMAN ASTROLOGERS AND THEIR INNOVATIONS 27

CHAPTER 8: ASTROLOGY IN ANCIENT GREEK MEDICINE AND HEALING 30

ASTROLOGICAL INFLUENCE ON MEDICAL PRACTICES........................ 30
CASE STUDIES OF ASTROLOGICAL HEALING 31

CHAPTER 9: NOTABLE ASTROLOGICAL TEXTS AND THEIR HISTORICAL
CONTEXTS 34

THE TETRABIBLOS AND ITS LEGACY....................................... 34

CHAPTER 10: THE RELATIONSHIP BETWEEN PHILOSOPHY AND
ASTROLOGY IN HELLENISTIC CULTURE 38

PHILOSOPHICAL SCHOOLS AND THEIR VIEWS ON ASTROLOGY.............. 38

ASTROLOGY'S ROLE IN PHILOSOPHICAL DISCOURSE 39

CHAPTER 11: SPECIFIC HISTORICAL EVENTS AND THEIR ASTROLOGICAL INTERPRETATIONS 42

1. FALL OF THE BERLIN WALL 43
   Chart Highlights: 45
2. APOLLO 11 MOON LANDING 46
   Chart Highlights: 48
3. SIGNING OF THE DECLARATION OF INDEPENDENCE 49
   Chart Highlights: 51
4. END OF WORLD WAR II (V-E DAY) 53
   Chart Highlights: 54
5. FALL OF CONSTANTINOPLE 56
   Chart Highlights: 57
6. ASSASSINATION OF ARCHDUKE FRANZ FERDINAND 59
   Chart Highlights: 61
7. GREAT FIRE OF LONDON 62
   Chart Highlights: 64
8. WOMEN'S SUFFRAGE GRANTED IN THE U.S. 65
   Chart Highlights: 67
9. FRENCH REVOLUTION BEGINS 69
   Chart Highlights: 70
10. HIROSHIMA ATOMIC BOMBING 71
    Chart Highlights: 73
11. DISCOVERY OF AMERICA BY COLUMBUS 74
    Chart Highlights: 76
12. MARTIN LUTHER'S 95 THESES PUBLISHED 78
    Chart Highlights: 79
13. SIGNING OF THE MAGNA CARTA 81
    Chart Highlights: 83
14. FIRST TELEPHONE CALL BY ALEXANDER GRAHAM BELL 84
    Chart Highlights: 86
15. SINKING OF THE TITANIC 87
    Chart Highlights: 89
16. MOON LANDING BY SOVIET LUNA 2 (FIRST MOON IMPACT) 90
    Chart Highlights: 92
17. INDIA GAINS INDEPENDENCE 93
    Chart Highlights: 95
18. WALL STREET STOCK MARKET CRASH (BLACK TUESDAY) 96
    Chart Highlights: 98
19. FIRST POWERED FLIGHT BY THE WRIGHT BROTHERS 99
    Chart Highlights: 101
20. FIRST USE OF THE INTERNET (ARPANET) 103
    Chart Highlights: 104

THEMES BETWEEN THE 20 HISTORICAL EVENTS 106

Transformation and Rebirth (Pluto and Scorpio Influences) *106*
Revolution and Breakthrough (Uranus and Aquarius Influences) *106*
Collective Identity and Unity (Jupiter and 11th House Focus) *106*
Authority and Structure (Saturn and Capricorn/Cancer Axes) *107*
Technology and Communication (Mercury and Gemini Influence) *107*
CONCLUSIONS *107*
Final Insight *108*

CHAPTER 12: CONCLUSION AND FUTURE DIRECTIONS IN HELLENISTIC ASTROLOGY **109**

CONTEMPORARY RELEVANCE AND APPLICATIONS 110

Chapter 1: Introduction to Hellenistic Astrology

Historical Overview

The Hellenistic period, spanning from the death of Alexander the Great in 323 BCE to the emergence of the Roman Empire in the 1st century BCE, marked a significant transformation in various fields, including astrology. This era witnessed the synthesis of Greek, Egyptian, and Babylonian astronomical and astrological traditions, which laid the groundwork for the development of Western astrology. The cultural exchanges that occurred during this time, particularly in cities such as Alexandria, facilitated the sharing of knowledge and methodologies, leading to the formulation of new astrological practices and theories that would influence generations of astrologers.

One of the most notable innovations during the Hellenistic period was the adoption of whole sign houses and the tropical zodiac, which became foundational to Western astrological practices. The whole sign house system simplifies the division of the sky into twelve equal segments, aligning each sign with a house, which contrasts with earlier methods that relied on the placement of the Ascendant. This approach offered a more intuitive understanding of planetary influences and made astrology more accessible to both practitioners and laypeople. The tropical zodiac, based on the seasons rather than the stars, further established a connection between celestial events and earthly phenomena, enhancing the practical application of astrology in various domains of life.

Key historical figures emerged during this period, whose contributions significantly shaped the course of astrology. Among them, Claudius Ptolemy stands out with his seminal work, the Tetrabiblos, which became a cornerstone for astrological thought for centuries. Ptolemy's systematic approach to astrology combined empirical observation with philosophical principles, establishing a framework that would be referenced and expanded upon by later scholars. Other astrological authorities, such as Vettius Valens and Dorotheus of Sidon, also played crucial roles in elaborating on techniques and interpretations, enriching the astrological corpus with diverse methodologies and insights.

Astrology's integration into ancient Greek political and medical practices further illustrates its importance in Hellenistic society. Political leaders often consulted astrologers to guide their decisions, believing that celestial alignments could provide insights into favorable times for warfare, governance, or public policy. This belief underscored astrology's perceived authority in matters of statecraft. Additionally, astrology found a significant place in the realm of medicine, where practitioners like Hippocrates and Galen incorporated astrological principles into their diagnostic and therapeutic approaches, suggesting that celestial influences could affect the health and temperament of individuals.

The legacy of Hellenistic astrology is evident in its enduring influence on Roman practices and beyond. As the Roman Empire expanded, it assimilated and adapted Hellenistic astrological teachings, which were disseminated throughout the empire. This integration not only solidified astrology's role in various aspects of daily life but also contributed to its evolution into the medieval and Renaissance periods. The relationship between astrology and philosophy during the Hellenistic era further fostered an environment where astrological inquiry was viewed as a legitimate pursuit of knowledge, setting the stage for the rich tapestry of astrological thought that would follow in Western history.

Key Concepts in Hellenistic Astrology

Key concepts in Hellenistic astrology form the foundation of astrological practices that have influenced both ancient and modern systems. Central to this framework is the use of whole sign houses, a method where each sign of the zodiac corresponds directly to a house in a natal chart. This approach simplifies the interpretation of astrological data, making it accessible and practical for astrologers of the time. Unlike the more complicated quadrant house systems that emerged later, whole sign houses provide a clear and immediate connection between the signs and their associated houses, enhancing the clarity of astrological predictions.

The tropical zodiac is another key element of Hellenistic astrology, determined by the position of the Sun relative to the Earth. This system reflects the cyclical nature of the seasons and is intimately linked to the agricultural calendar of the ancient Greeks. By aligning astrological phenomena with seasonal changes, practitioners were able to create a more practical framework that resonated with everyday life. This connection to the natural world not only informed astrological interpretations but also reinforced the significance of celestial events in guiding human affairs.

The influence of the Hellenistic period on astrology practices cannot be overstated. This era saw the synthesis of various astrological traditions, including Babylonian and Egyptian influences, leading to a more comprehensive system of understanding celestial influences. Hellenistic astrologers such as Ptolemy and Vettius Valens contributed significantly to the codification of astrological principles, merging observational techniques with theoretical constructs. Their works laid the groundwork for future astrological practices and established a legacy that would endure for centuries.

Astrology in ancient Greece was not merely a tool for personal insight; it played a pivotal role in political decision-making. Leaders consulted astrologers to gauge the auspiciousness of certain actions, such as military campaigns or the timing of public events. This reliance on celestial guidance illustrates the deep-seated belief in the interconnectedness of cosmic forces and human affairs. The interpretation of planetary alignments was often seen as a reflection of the will of the gods, providing rulers with a divine mandate or warning that could impact the fate of their city-states.

The impact of Hellenistic astrology extended beyond Greece into Roman practices, shaping the astrological landscape of the Empire. Roman astrologers adopted and adapted Hellenistic techniques, integrating them into their own cultural and philosophical contexts. Texts such as the "Tetrabiblos" by Ptolemy remained influential, bridging the gap between the two civilizations.

Furthermore, the application of astrology in medicine during this period highlighted its multifaceted role, as practitioners sought to align healing practices with celestial rhythms. The integration of astrology and medicine in Hellenistic culture reflects a holistic understanding of health, emphasizing the significance of the cosmos in the well-being of individuals and society at large.

Chapter 2: The Development of Whole Sign Houses

Origins and Evolution

The origins of Hellenistic astrology can be traced back to the confluence of various ancient traditions, particularly those of Babylonian, Egyptian, and Greek astrological practices. This synthesis occurred during the Hellenistic period, which began with the conquests of Alexander the Great in the 4th century BCE. The spread of Greek culture throughout the Mediterranean and Near East facilitated the exchange of astrological knowledge. Babylonian astrology, with its complex system of celestial omens and planetary movements, significantly influenced the development of Hellenistic practices. Egyptian contributions, particularly through the priestly class in Alexandria, introduced the concept of decans and the integration of astrology within religious and medical contexts.

As Hellenistic astrology evolved, it embraced a more systematic approach to celestial interpretation. The introduction of the whole sign house system represented a pivotal shift, allowing astrologers to assign houses to zodiac signs in a straightforward manner. This system simplified the calculations and interpretations of horoscopes, making astrology more accessible to practitioners and their clients. The tropical zodiac, aligned with the seasons rather than the constellations, further distinguished Hellenistic astrology from its predecessors. This development reflected a growing understanding of the relationship between celestial phenomena and earthly events, emphasizing the cyclical nature of time and the influence of the cosmos on human affairs.

Key historical figures emerged during this period, each contributing to the rich tapestry of Hellenistic astrology. Notable astrologers such as Ptolemy, Vettius Valens, and Dorotheus of Sidon authored texts that would become foundational for future generations. Ptolemy's "Tetrabiblos" systematically compiled astrological knowledge and made significant contributions to the understanding of planetary aspects and their effects on human life. Vettius

Valens, through his "Anthology," provided practical examples of astrological techniques, showcasing diverse methods of interpretation. These texts not only codified existing knowledge but also influenced Roman astrology and later Western practices, solidifying the Hellenistic legacy.

Astrology's role in ancient Greek political decisions cannot be understated. Leaders and statesmen often consulted astrologers to gain insights into the timing of significant events, such as wars, elections, and public projects. The belief that celestial events could foreshadow earthly outcomes reinforced the authority of astrologers in political spheres. This relationship between astrology and governance was particularly evident during the Hellenistic period, where the integration of astrological advice into statecraft reflected the prevailing worldview that the cosmos held sway over human affairs. As such, astrology became an essential tool for those in power, influencing decisions that would shape the course of history.

The impact of Hellenistic astrology extended beyond politics into various aspects of daily life, including medicine and healing. Ancient practitioners often incorporated astrological principles into their medical practices, believing that celestial alignments could affect health and wellbeing. The alignment of planets at the time of a person's birth was thought to influence their physical and mental constitution, leading to personalized healing approaches. This intersection of astrology and medicine further exemplified the holistic worldview of the Hellenistic period, where the cosmos, nature, and human experience were interconnected. As Hellenistic astrology continued to evolve, its principles were absorbed into Roman practices and later European astrology, ensuring its relevance and influence for centuries to come.

Comparison with Other House Systems

The exploration of house systems in astrology has led to significant divergences in practice and interpretation, particularly when comparing the Whole Sign House system prevalent in Hellenistic astrology with other prevalent systems. The Whole Sign system, where each house corresponds to an entire sign of the zodiac, offers a seamless approach to delineating a chart, emphasizing the importance of signs as foundational units. This contrasts sharply with the more commonly used Placidus system, which divides the celestial sphere into unequal segments based on the time of birth, potentially leading to complex interpretations that can vary significantly depending on the precise birth time.

Another notable comparison arises with the Equal House system, which, like Whole Sign Houses, assigns an entire sign to each house but is determined differently. In the Equal House system, the Ascendant marks the beginning of the first house, with each subsequent house corresponding directly to the signs that follow. This approach echoes the simplicity of the Whole Sign method, but can lead to discrepancies in specific chart readings, particularly for individuals whose Ascendant is near the cusp of a sign. Both systems prioritize the significance of the rising sign, yet the impact on chart interpretation can be profound, revealing different layers of meaning in the same celestial configuration.

The Hellenistic approach, with its roots in ancient Greek philosophy, posits a more holistic view of astrological influence, which is often at odds with the more fragmented nature of modern systems. The integration of philosophy and astrology in Hellenistic culture provided a framework that viewed the cosmos as a unified whole, where the planets and the signs collaboratively influenced human affairs. This contrasts with the contemporary tendency to treat astrological elements in isolation, which can obscure the interconnectedness emphasized by Hellenistic astrologers. Such philosophical underpinnings are essential for understanding how historical figures in this period approached astrology, as their methods were deeply intertwined with their metaphysical beliefs.

In examining the influence of Hellenistic astrology on later Roman practices, it becomes evident that the foundation laid by earlier astrologers was built upon in various ways. While the Romans adopted many Hellenistic techniques, they also introduced modifications that reflect their cultural values and societal structure. For instance, Roman astrology often placed greater emphasis on predictive techniques and personal fate, diverging from the more collective interpretations found in Hellenistic texts. This shift illustrates how the same astrological principles can evolve to serve different societal needs, highlighting the adaptability and resilience of astrological systems across cultures and epochs.

The interplay between astrology and medicine in Hellenistic practices further accentuates the distinctiveness of the Whole Sign House system. Ancient Greek physicians often employed astrological insights to guide medical treatments, relying on the belief that celestial configurations could influence health outcomes. In this context, the Whole Sign Houses provided a straightforward method for determining the houses associated with various bodily parts and functions. This contrasts with later systems that might complicate the relationship between astrology and medicine, underscoring the practical applications of Hellenistic astrology in everyday life and its enduring legacy in the integration of spiritual and physical well-being.

Chapter 3: The Tropical Zodiac in Hellenistic Astrology

Definition and Significance

In the context of Hellenistic astrology, the definition of astrology extends beyond mere horoscopic practice; it embodies a comprehensive system that intertwines celestial phenomena with human experience. At its core, astrology in this era is defined as the study of the movements and positions of celestial bodies, interpreted to understand their influence on earthly events and individual destinies. This period marks a significant evolution in astrological practices, particularly with the introduction of whole sign houses and the use of the tropical zodiac, which provided astrologers with more systematic frameworks for interpretation and prediction. The methodologies developed during this time laid the groundwork for future astrological traditions, establishing an enduring legacy in both Western astrology and beyond.

The significance of Hellenistic astrology cannot be overstated, as it represents a pivotal moment in the history of astrological thought, where theory and practice began to coalesce into a more structured discipline. This era saw the integration of various philosophical schools, such as Stoicism and Neoplatonism, which deeply influenced astrological interpretation and its applications. The Hellenistic astrologers' ability to synthesize these philosophical ideas with empirical observations of the heavens created a unique framework that emphasized the interconnectedness of the cosmos and human affairs. This holistic approach not only enhanced the predictive capabilities of astrology but also elevated its status as a respected intellectual pursuit.

Moreover, the Hellenistic period was marked by significant historical events that shaped the practice of astrology, including the rise of the Roman Empire and the spread of Greek culture throughout the Mediterranean. As astrology became intertwined with political decisions, rulers and statesmen relied on astrological guidance to make informed choices that would impact governance and military strategies. The role of astrology in these political contexts highlights its importance as a tool for power and authority, demonstrating how celestial phenomena were believed to reflect and influence terrestrial governance. This relationship between astrology and politics underscored its societal relevance, fostering a deeper appreciation for its predictive insights. Key historical figures emerged during this period, each contributing uniquely to the development of astrological thought. Prominent astrologers such as Ptolemy, Vettius Valens, and Dorotheus of Sidon offered seminal texts that outlined principles of interpretation, techniques for chart construction, and methods for integrating astrological insights into various aspects of life, including medicine and healing. Their contributions not only advanced the practice itself but also provided a rich historical context that informs modern astrological practices. The works of these figures are essential for understanding how Hellenistic astrology evolved and adapted over time, resonating through subsequent generations of astrologers.

Finally, the interplay between astrology and other fields during the Hellenistic period, such as medicine and philosophy, underscores its multifaceted significance. Astrological concepts were employed in medical contexts, with practitioners using celestial alignments to diagnose and treat ailments, reflecting a belief in the cosmic roots of health and disease. The philosophical underpinnings of astrology during this time encouraged a dialogue between the heavens and human understanding, fostering a deeper exploration of existence and the nature of reality. This relationship enriched both astrology and philosophy, creating a legacy that continues to influence contemporary astrological practices and thought, emphasizing the enduring importance of Hellenistic astrology in the broader tapestry of human knowledge.

Differences Between Tropical and Sidereal Zodiac

The differences between the tropical and sidereal zodiac systems are foundational to understanding the evolution of astrology during the Hellenistic period and its subsequent influence on Western practices. The tropical zodiac, which is prevalent in Western astrology, is based on the seasons and the relationship of the Earth to the Sun. It divides the ecliptic into twelve equal parts, aligning the start of Aries with the vernal equinox. In contrast, the sidereal zodiac, which originated in ancient Babylon and was later adopted in various forms throughout the Hellenistic world, is based on the actual positions of constellations in the sky. This system aligns zodiac signs with specific constellations, thus reflecting the fixed positions of stars.

The significance of these differing systems becomes evident when examining their implications for astrological interpretation. The tropical zodiac emphasizes the solar year and the changing seasons, which aligns with the ancient Greeks' focus on agricultural cycles and their direct influence on societal activities and political decisions. For instance, the timing of festivals and harvests was often dictated by the tropical zodiac, creating a rhythm that governed civic life. Conversely, the sidereal zodiac's focus on the constellations offered a more cosmic perspective, allowing astrologers to consider fixed stars and their influence on individual destinies, thereby enriching personal astrology.

Moreover, the historical context of these zodiacs reflects broader philosophical and cultural shifts in Hellenistic society. The tropical zodiac's establishment during the late Hellenistic period coincided with the rise of philosophical schools, such as Stoicism and Neoplatonism, which emphasized the relationship between humanity and the divine order. This philosophical backdrop supported the idea that human events are influenced by celestial phenomena, reinforcing the importance of the tropical zodiac in political and medical astrology. In contrast, the sidereal zodiac maintained its relevance through its ties to older Babylonian traditions, which were often viewed with a sense of nostalgia and reverence, especially as Rome absorbed Hellenistic ideas.

The impact of these differing zodiac systems also extended to key historical figures in astrology, whose contributions shaped the understanding and application of these frameworks. Prominent astrologers like Ptolemy utilized the tropical zodiac in his seminal work, the Tetrabiblos, advocating for its use in predictive astrology and demonstrating its practical applications in political and medical contexts. At the same time, figures who adhered to the sidereal system, such as Vettius Valens, emphasized its astrological depth through detailed interpretations of fixed stars, providing a rich tapestry of astrological practice that influenced later generations.

Ultimately, the divergent approaches of the tropical and sidereal zodiacs reflect the dynamic interplay between cultural, philosophical, and astronomical developments in the Hellenistic period. This divergence not only illustrates the adaptability of astrology to the needs and beliefs of its practitioners but also underscores the lasting impact of these systems on subsequent astrological traditions in the Roman Empire and beyond. Understanding these differences is essential for modern astrologers seeking to appreciate the historical context and evolution of astrological practices that continue to shape contemporary interpretations today.

Chapter 4: Key Historical Figures in Hellenistic Astrology

Ptolemy and His Contributions

Ptolemy, a prominent figure in the realm of Hellenistic astrology, made significant contributions that shaped the discipline and influenced its evolution. His work, particularly in the compilation of astrological texts, served as a cornerstone for both contemporary and future astrologers. The most notable of these texts is the "Tetrabiblos," which synthesizes various astrological traditions and presents a coherent framework for understanding celestial influences on earthly events. Ptolemy's systematic approach to astrology emphasized the importance of the individual's birth chart and the use of planetary positions to interpret personal destinies, thus establishing a foundation for the practice of natal astrology that is still relevant today.

One of Ptolemy's key contributions was his advocacy for the use of the tropical zodiac, which aligns the zodiac signs with the seasons rather than the constellations. This approach allowed astrologers to create horoscopes that reflect seasonal changes and agricultural cycles, making astrology more applicable to the lives of individuals in an agrarian society. Ptolemy argued that the tropical zodiac offered a more consistent framework for interpreting celestial movements, thereby influencing subsequent astrological practices in both the Hellenistic world and later in Roman astrology. His work illustrated the adaptability of astrological methods in response to cultural and astronomical developments.

Furthermore, Ptolemy's emphasis on the mathematical and astronomical underpinnings of astrology was revolutionary. He incorporated geometric principles and observational data into astrological calculations, promoting a more scientific approach to the discipline. This integration of mathematics and astrology not only enhanced the accuracy of astrological predictions but also elevated the status of astrology as a scholarly pursuit. Ptolemy's insistence on rigorous methodologies set a precedent that would guide future astrologers,

13

urging them to base their practices on empirical observations rather than mere tradition.

The influence of Ptolemy extended beyond astrology into the realms of medicine and political decision-making in ancient Greece. He believed that celestial phenomena could be correlated with health and well-being, a notion that resonated with contemporary medical practices that sought to align treatments with astrological insights. His work provided practitioners with a framework to consider the timing of medical interventions based on astrological conditions, thus intertwining astrology with healing practices. In politics, Ptolemy's astrological principles were utilized to guide decisions, with leaders consulting astrological predictions to determine auspicious times for actions, thereby underscoring astrology's role in governance.

Ptolemy's legacy is evident in the enduring impact of his writings and methodologies on subsequent generations of astrologers. The "Tetrabiblos" became a foundational text for both Islamic and medieval European astrology, demonstrating the cross-cultural influence of his ideas. His integration of philosophy and astrology also paved the way for a deeper exploration of the relationship between celestial phenomena and human affairs, a theme that would resonate throughout the history of astrology. Ptolemy's contributions not only solidified the practice of astrology during the Hellenistic period but also ensured its relevance and adaptability in the centuries to follow.

Vettius Valens: A Pioneering Astrologer

Vettius Valens stands as a pivotal figure in the realm of Hellenistic astrology, renowned for his comprehensive work that encapsulated and expanded upon the astrological knowledge of his time. Active during the second century CE, Valens' contributions are most notably found in his seminal text, the Anthology, which is a compilation of astrological techniques, interpretations, and historical insights. This work not only reflects the sophistication of Hellenistic astrology but also serves as a crucial link between earlier traditions and the subsequent evolution of astrological practices in the Roman period. Valens' emphasis on empirical observation and the integration of various astrological methodologies marked a significant departure from the more rigid frameworks that preceded him.

Valens' methodology was characterized by his use of whole sign houses, a system that allowed for a more intultlve interpretation of the natal chart. This approach simplified the complex calculations required in earlier systems, making astrology more accessible to practitioners and clients alike. His preference for the tropical zodiac also highlighted a shift towards a more seasonal understanding of astrology, aligning celestial events with earthly phenomena. This connection between the heavens and human affairs encapsulated the Hellenistic worldview, where astrology was seen not merely as a predictive tool but as a means of understanding one's place in the cosmos. In addition to technical innovations, Valens emphasized the practical applications of astrology in various aspects of life, including medicine and politics. His work often intertwined astrological insights with healing practices, reflecting the belief that celestial influences could directly affect physical well-being. This integration of astrology into medical contexts illustrates the broad acceptance of astrological principles in Hellenistic society and their perceived relevance in everyday life, reinforcing the notion that astrology was a vital component of ancient Greek medicine.

Furthermore, Valens' writings provide invaluable insights into the political landscape of his time. He recognized the influence of celestial events on significant political decisions, advising rulers and leaders based on astrological forecasts. This intersection of astrology and politics not only underscores the importance of astrological counsel in governance but also highlights the broader societal implications of astrological practices. Valens' observations contribute to our understanding of how astrology was utilized as a tool for navigating political complexities and asserting authority.

The legacy of Vettius Valens is profound, influencing subsequent generations of astrologers and shaping the trajectory of Western astrology. His integration of empirical observation with theoretical frameworks laid the groundwork for later astrological developments. The Anthology remains a critical text for historians and practitioners alike, offering a window into the astrological thought of the Hellenistic period. Valens' pioneering spirit and dedication to the discipline continue to inspire modern astrologers, affirming his status as a foundational figure in the history of astrology.

Other Influential Astrologers

Astrology in the Hellenistic period was shaped not only by foundational figures like Ptolemy and Hipparchus but also by a broader array of influential astrologers whose contributions enriched the discipline. One such figure was Vettius Valens, whose work, the Anthology, serves as a vital source for understanding the practical application of astrology in the second century CE. Valens emphasized the importance of personal experience and observation in astrological practice, diverging from earlier theoretical approaches. His detailed case studies highlight the significance of individual horoscopes, providing insights into how astrology was used to navigate personal destinies, societal roles, and even political ambitions in a turbulent era.

Another noteworthy astrologer from this period is Porphyry, a philosopher and student of Plotinus, who contributed to the integration of astrology with Neoplatonism. His work, the Introductory Commentary on Ptolemy's Tetrabiblos, illustrates how astrological concepts were interwoven with philosophical thought. Porphyry's emphasis on the correspondence between celestial movements and human affairs reflects the broader Hellenistic belief in a cosmos imbued with meaning. This philosophical underpinning not only legitimized astrology as a scholarly pursuit but also influenced how practitioners interpreted astrological signs and their implications for human behavior and decision-making.

Firmicus Maternus, writing in the fourth century CE, further expanded the astrological tradition with his magnum opus, the Mathesis. His work marked a significant shift, focusing on the moral and ethical dimensions of astrological practice. Maternus argued for the alignment of astrological understanding with Christian thought, attempting to reconcile the two systems. His writings demonstrate how astrology adapted to the changing religious landscape of the

Roman Empire, reflecting the ongoing dialogue between ancient beliefs and emerging Christian doctrines. This melding of astrology with moral philosophy and theology underscored the importance of ethical considerations in astrological predictions and practice.

In addition to these figures, the role of astrologers in political decision-making cannot be overlooked. Astrologers were often consulted by rulers and politicians, who relied on their insights to guide significant actions and policy decisions. The intertwining of astrology with governance highlights its perceived authority and the trust placed in astrological predictions. Historical accounts illustrate how astrological readings were used to determine the most auspicious times for military campaigns, public events, and even the selection of leaders, reflecting the profound influence of astrology on the sociopolitical landscape of Hellenistic societies.

Lastly, the impact of these influential astrologers extended beyond the Hellenistic world, shaping astrological practices in Roman culture and beyond. Their texts and teachings laid the groundwork for later developments in astrological thought, influencing both medieval and Renaissance astrology. The blending of Hellenistic astrology with other traditions, such as Roman and later Islamic astrological practices, created a rich tapestry of astrological knowledge that continues to resonate today. The legacy of these key figures is thus not only found in their individual contributions but also in the broader evolution of astrology as a discipline that bridges various cultures and philosophical frameworks.

Chapter 5: The Influence of the Hellenistic Period on Astrology Practices

Cultural Exchanges and Their Impact

Cultural exchanges during the Hellenistic period significantly influenced the development of astrology, integrating various philosophical and scientific traditions. As Alexander the Great expanded his empire, he facilitated interactions between Greek, Egyptian, Babylonian, and Persian cultures. This fusion of ideas led to the synthesis of astrological practices that drew from diverse sources, enriching the astrological landscape. The incorporation of Babylonian techniques, such as the zodiacal system and planetary periods, into Greek astrology exemplifies how cultural exchanges allowed for the cross-pollination of astrological methods, resulting in a more robust and versatile practice.

The impact of these exchanges is most evident in the adoption of the whole sign house system, which emerged as a significant innovation in Hellenistic astrology. This system simplified the interpretation of astrological charts by assigning each sign of the zodiac as a house, promoting a more intuitive understanding of planetary positions and their influences. The migration of ideas from the East played a crucial role in this development, demonstrating how the amalgamation of different cultural perspectives can lead to advancements in knowledge. Astrologers of the time could draw upon a richer set of tools for chart interpretation, enhancing their ability to analyze celestial phenomena and make predictions.

Moreover, the philosophical underpinnings of astrology were deeply affected by these cultural exchanges. The integration of Platonic and Stoic thought with astrological principles led to a more profound exploration of the relationship between the cosmos and human existence. Astrologers began to emphasize the interconnectedness of the universe, which not only influenced astrological practice but also shaped broader philosophical discussions about fate, free will, and the nature of reality. This philosophical dialogue underscored the role of astrology in guiding political decisions, as leaders sought astrological counsel to navigate complex social and political landscapes.

The influence of Hellenistic astrology extended beyond Greece, permeating Roman practices and shaping astrological thought in the West. As Roman scholars encountered Hellenistic texts and techniques, they adopted and adapted these methods, creating a unique blend that would dominate astrological practice throughout the Roman Empire. This transfer of knowledge highlights the dynamic nature of cultural exchanges, illustrating how ideas can transcend geographic and cultural boundaries to shape practices in new contexts. The Roman adaptation of Hellenistic astrology not only preserved these traditions but also contributed to their evolution.

In medicine and healing, the impact of cultural exchanges can be seen in the integration of astrological principles with medical practices. Hellenistic physicians, influenced by both Greek and Egyptian traditions, utilized astrology to understand the timing of treatments and the influence of celestial bodies on health. This approach illustrated a holistic view of wellness, where astrological insights informed medical decisions. The blending of astrology with medical practices exemplifies the profound ways in which cultural exchanges enriched various aspects of life in the Hellenistic world, creating a legacy that would influence future generations of astrologers and healers.

The Integration of Astronomy and Astrology

The integration of astronomy and astrology during the Hellenistic period marked a significant evolution in the understanding and practice of celestial observation and interpretation. Astronomers of the time, such as Hipparchus, laid the groundwork for precise celestial measurements, including the development of star catalogs and the refinement of the geocentric model of the universe. This empirical approach to the heavens provided astrologers with the necessary tools to correlate celestial movements with terrestrial events. The alignment of astronomical observations with astrological applications not only enhanced the predictive capabilities of astrology but also established it as a respected discipline within the broader context of Hellenistic science.

As astrology became increasingly sophisticated, it began to reflect the cultural and philosophical currents of the Hellenistic world. The merging of Platonic and Aristotelian thought with astrological principles gave rise to a worldview in which celestial bodies were seen as influencing human affairs and natural phenomena. This philosophical undercurrent was significant in shaping the astrological methodologies that emerged during this period, particularly the adoption of whole sign houses and the tropical zodiac. By framing astrological interpretation within the context of philosophical inquiry, practitioners were able to elevate the status of astrology, positioning it not merely as a form of divination but as a legitimate means of understanding the cosmos and its influence on human existence.

Key historical figures from the Hellenistic era played pivotal roles in this integration. Claudius Ptolemy, for instance, synthesized astronomical knowledge and astrological practice in his seminal work, the Tetrabiblos. Ptolemy's writings not only codified existing astrological traditions but also provided a systematic framework for interpreting planetary positions and their implications for individual destinies and societal events. His work served as a bridge between astronomy and astrology, demonstrating that the study of the heavens could yield insights into the human condition and the unfolding of historical events.

The role of astrology in ancient Greek political decisions further exemplifies the intimate relationship between astronomy and astrology. Rulers and statesmen often consulted astrologers to inform key decisions, believing that celestial alignments could presage favorable or unfavorable outcomes in governance and warfare. This practice underscored the necessity for astrologers to possess a solid understanding of astronomy, as accurate celestial calculations were essential for making informed predictions. The reliance on astrological guidance in political contexts illustrates how deeply embedded astrology was in the fabric of Hellenistic society, influencing not just individual lives but also the course of history itself.

The impact of Hellenistic astrology extended beyond Greek borders, significantly influencing Roman astrological practices as well. The Romans adopted and adapted many Hellenistic astrological concepts, integrating them into their own cultural and political frameworks. This cross-cultural exchange enriched both traditions, leading to the development of new techniques and interpretations that would resonate throughout the centuries. The enduring legacy of Hellenistic astrology is evident in its foundational texts and practices, which continue to inform contemporary astrological thought and highlight the lasting connection between astronomy and astrology as intertwined disciplines in the understanding of the cosmos and human experience.

Chapter 6: Astrology and Political Decisions in Ancient Greece

The Role of Astrology in Statecraft

The role of astrology in statecraft during the Hellenistic period is a compelling intersection of celestial observation and political decision-making. Astrologers were often consulted by rulers and officials, who believed that the positions of celestial bodies could provide guidance on crucial matters affecting the state. The practice of astrology was deeply embedded within the political fabric of Hellenistic society, where leaders sought to align their strategies with the cosmic order. This reliance on astrology was not merely superstition; it was rooted in philosophical traditions that viewed the universe as an interconnected whole, where human affairs were influenced by celestial movements.

Astrological expertise was particularly sought during significant political events, such as the ascension of a new ruler or the commencement of military campaigns. Rulers like Ptolemy and Seleucus relied on astrologers to determine auspicious times for decisions and actions. The practice of electional astrology, which identifies favorable moments for specific endeavors, became crucial for ensuring success in governance and warfare. The belief that celestial alignments could herald either prosperity or disaster led to a heightened sensitivity among political leaders to the timing of their actions, embedding astrology into the core of statecraft.

Astrology also played a pivotal role in international diplomacy. Rulers would often consult astrological charts to assess the compatibility of their reign with neighboring states, influencing decisions on alliances and conflicts. This practice was not confined to any one nation; rather, it was a shared understanding across Hellenistic territories, reflecting a broader cultural appreciation for the cosmos. The interplay of astrology and diplomacy illustrated a sophisticated approach to governance, where leaders sought to harmonize their ambitions with the divine order as perceived through the stars.

The influence of prominent astrologers, such as Hipparchus and Ptolemy, further solidified the role of astrology In political spheres. Their writings not only contributed to astrological theory but also provided practical frameworks that could be applied to real-world situations. Texts such as the Tetrabiblos offered rulers insights into astrological interpretations of their own horoscopes and those of their adversaries. This exchange of astrological knowledge across courts and scholars facilitated a rich dialogue that informed statecraft, enabling leaders to navigate complex political landscapes with a celestial compass.

Ultimately, the integration of astrology in Hellenistic statecraft underscores a broader philosophical perspective that viewed the cosmos as a dynamic force influencing human affairs. The period's prominent philosophers and astrologers shared a conviction that understanding the heavens could yield insights into earthly power dynamics. As such, astrology was not merely a method of divination but a sophisticated tool for governance that shaped the decisions of some of history's most notable figures. This enduring legacy of astrology in political decision-making continued to influence subsequent civilizations, marking a significant chapter in the history of both astrology and statecraft.

Notable Political Figures and Their Astrological Consultations

Notable political figures in ancient Greece and Rome often sought astrological guidance to inform their decisions and strategies. The practice of astrology during the Hellenistic period was deeply intertwined with governance, as leaders believed that celestial phenomena could provide insights into the favor of the gods and the timing of their political maneuvers. Key figures, such as Alexander the Great and Julius Caesar, utilized astrologers to forecast the outcomes of their campaigns and to enhance their authority among the populace. Their reliance on astrological consultations illustrates the significant role astrology played in shaping political landscapes during this era.

Alexander the Great, for instance, was known to have consulted with the famous astrologer Chaldean, who advised him on the auspicious timing of his military campaigns. This consultation was not merely a matter of superstition; it was a strategic maneuver that helped him achieve remarkable successes across vast territories. The astrological charts drawn up for Alexander provided him with insights about potential challenges and victories, thereby reinforcing his image as a leader favored by the divine. His use of astrology can be seen as a reflection of the broader cultural belief in the power of the stars to influence human affairs.

Julius Caesar similarly recognized the importance of astrology in his political life. His interactions with the astrologer Spurinna prior to the Ides of March highlight a critical moment in Roman history. Spurinna warned Caesar to be wary of the approaching date, which foreshadowed his assassination. Although Caesar dismissed the warning, the event underscores the pervasive belief that astrology could illuminate future dangers. This incident not only illustrates the personal stakes involved but also emphasizes how astrology was woven into the fabric of political decision-making in Rome.

The legacy of these practices extended beyond individual leaders, influencing the broader political culture of both Greece and Rome. The integration of astrological advice into governance established a precedent for future rulers, who continued to rely on astrologers to navigate the complexities of leadership. This trend persisted through the Hellenistic period and into the Roman Empire, where astrology became an essential tool for understanding public sentiment and political timing. The consultation of astrologers by political leaders signified a merging of celestial knowledge with earthly power, echoing the belief that the heavens and human destiny were inextricably linked.

In conclusion, the consultations of notable political figures with astrologers illuminate the profound impact of astrology on governance during the Hellenistic period. The intertwining of astrological practices with political decisions not only shaped the actions of individuals like Alexander and Caesar but also laid the groundwork for the institutionalization of astrology in governance. As historians and astrologers reflect on these historical contexts, it becomes evident that the influence of astrology extended far beyond mere prediction; it was a vital component of the political machinery that defined the era.

Chapter 7: The Impact of Hellenistic Astrology on Roman Practices

Adoption and Adaptation in Roman Society

Adoption and adaptation of Hellenistic astrology within Roman society illustrate the dynamic interplay between cultures during this transitional period. As the Roman Empire expanded, it encountered the diverse traditions and intellectual practices of the Hellenistic world. Astrological concepts originating from Greek thinkers, such as Ptolemy and Hipparchus, were integrated into Roman life, significantly influencing various aspects of society, from politics to medicine. This interchange was not merely one-sided; rather, it involved a complex negotiation where Roman practitioners adapted Hellenistic theories to fit their own cultural and social contexts.

The Roman adaptation of astrology was marked by the integration of local beliefs and practices, allowing astrology to resonate with Roman values. Unlike the Greeks, who often focused on astrology's philosophical dimensions, Romans emphasized its practical applications. Astrologers in Rome began to tailor astrological advice to suit the demands of their society, particularly in matters of governance and personal affairs. This pragmatic approach fostered a burgeoning interest in astrological predictions related to political events, military endeavors, and even public health. As a result, astrology became a vital tool for Roman leaders seeking to justify their decisions and gain popular support.

One key aspect of this adaptation was the incorporation of the whole sign house system and the tropical zodiac. While the Greeks primarily utilized the equal house system, Roman astrologers found the whole sign house approach appealing due to its simplicity and ease of interpretation. This shift not only streamlined astrological readings but also made astrology more accessible to a broader audience. Moreover, the tropical zodiac, based on the seasons rather than the fixed stars, resonated with Roman agricultural cycles and societal rhythms, further embedding astrology within the everyday lives of the populace.

Astrology's role in Roman political decision-making exemplified its significance within the fabric of society. High-ranking officials and emperors often consulted astrologers before making crucial decisions, reflecting a deep-seated belief in celestial influences on human affairs. Prominent figures like Julius Caesar and Augustus employed astrologers to gain insights into the future, solidifying astrology's status as a legitimate and respected practice in political circles. This reliance on astrological counsel not only shaped individual destinies but also influenced the trajectory of the Roman Empire itself.

The intertwining of astrology with Roman medicine and healing practices also highlights its pervasive influence. Medical practitioners began to incorporate astrological timing into their treatments, adhering to the belief that celestial events could affect health and wellness. Astrological texts became essential resources for physicians, guiding them in diagnosing and treating ailments based on the positions of celestial bodies. This synthesis of astrology and medicine not only enriched Roman medical practice but also demonstrated the enduring legacy of Hellenistic thought, as it evolved to meet the needs of Roman society while maintaining its foundational principles.

Key Roman Astrologers and Their Innovations

The transition of astrology from the Hellenistic period to Roman society marked a significant evolution in astrological practices, with several key figures emerging as pioneers in this field. One of the most influential Roman astrologers was Vettius Valens, who built upon the foundations laid by his Hellenistic predecessors. Valens' extensive work, the Anthology, compiled various astrological traditions and emphasized the importance of individualized horoscopy. His innovative approach to natal astrology underscored the significance of personal destinies shaped by celestial influences, a concept that resonated deeply within Roman culture.

Another prominent figure was Firmicus Maternus, whose treatise, Mathesis, synthesized earlier astrological doctrines while introducing a more systematic methodology. Firmicus emphasized the use of the whole sign house system, which represented a shift from the more complex techniques of earlier astrologers. This approach simplified the interpretation of horoscopes, making astrology more accessible to practitioners and the general public alike. His work not only reinforced the significance of astrology in personal and political contexts but also helped solidify its status as a legitimate scholarly discipline in Rome.

Manilius, a poet and astrologer, also played a crucial role in the Roman adaptation of astrology through his work, Astronomica. This comprehensive poem merged astronomical and astrological concepts, providing a unique perspective on the relationship between the stars and human affairs. Manilius' innovative use of poetic form allowed him to articulate complex astrological ideas in a way that was both engaging and accessible. His integration of philosophical elements into astrology highlighted the discipline's connection to broader intellectual currents of the time, particularly Stoicism and Neoplatonism.

Moreover, the astrologer Claudius Ptolemy significantly impacted Roman astrology with his seminal work, Tetrabiblos. Ptolemy's text is often regarded as one of the most authoritative astrological works of antiquity, presenting a comprehensive system that combined mathematical precision with practical application. His innovations included a rigorous approach to planetary relationships and an emphasis on the tropical zodiac, which represented a departure from earlier sidereal practices. Ptolemy's influence extended beyond astrology into fields such as geography and astronomy, showcasing the interdisciplinary nature of knowledge during the Hellenistic period.

The contributions of these Roman astrologers not only enriched the astrological tradition but also influenced various aspects of Roman life, including politics, medicine, and philosophy. Their innovations laid the groundwork for future developments in astrology, establishing frameworks that would be utilized by later scholars and practitioners. By integrating Hellenistic astrological concepts with Roman sensibilities, these key figures helped to shape the astrological landscape, ensuring its relevance and application in both personal and societal contexts.

Chapter 8: Astrology in Ancient Greek Medicine and Healing

Astrological Influence on Medical Practices

Astrological influence on medical practices during the Hellenistic period is a fascinating intersection of celestial observation and bodily health. The ancient Greeks believed that the positions of the stars and planets at the time of a person's birth could significantly affect their health and predisposition to certain ailments. This belief was not merely speculative; it was grounded in a rich tradition of astrological texts that detailed the connections between celestial phenomena and human physiology. Practitioners of astrology and medicine often collaborated, using astrological charts to diagnose and prescribe treatments that were believed to be aligned with the cosmic influences affecting the individual.

The prominent figure of Hippocrates, often regarded as the father of medicine, exemplifies the integration of astrology into medical practices. His teachings acknowledged the significance of the seasons and celestial bodies in relation to health. Hippocratic texts suggested that different diseases were influenced by the positions of the planets, particularly in relation to the elements of earth, air, fire, and water. This holistic approach underscored the belief that understanding one's astrological profile could enhance the efficacy of medical treatments, as practitioners sought to harmonize their patients' conditions with cosmic rhythms.

Astrology played a crucial role in the development of medical theories and practices during the Hellenistic era. The concept of the four humors—blood, phlegm, black bile, and yellow bile—was often linked to astrological signs. Each humor was associated with specific zodiac signs, seasons, and planetary influences, which meant that a physician could tailor treatments based on this astrological framework. For instance, a patient born under a fire sign might be treated differently from one born under a water sign, with remedies chosen to address the elemental imbalances thought to be exacerbated by astrological conditions.

Moreover, astrological charts were frequently utilized to determine the most auspicious times for surgical procedures or the administration of remedies. Medical practitioners would consult the positions of the moon and planets to identify favorable moments for intervention, believing that the alignment of celestial bodies could enhance recovery and minimize complications. This practice was not limited to medicine alone; it extended to various aspects of daily life, reflecting the pervasive nature of astrology in Hellenistic culture. The legacy of astrological influence on medical practices persisted even as the Hellenistic period transitioned into Roman times. Roman physicians, like Galen, continued to incorporate astrological principles into their work, ensuring that the relationship between astrology and medicine endured for centuries. The integration of these disciplines shaped the medical landscape, influencing not only treatments but also the philosophical underpinnings of health and wellness. As such, the astrological perspective on medicine during the Hellenistic era offers a profound understanding of how ancient cultures perceived the interconnectedness of the cosmos and human life, a theme that remains relevant in contemporary discussions of holistic health practices.

Case Studies of Astrological Healing

Astrological healing in the Hellenistic period reflects a profound integration of astrological principles with medical practices. Case studies from this era illustrate how practitioners employed astrology not only to diagnose ailments but also to devise treatment plans. One notable case involves the physician Asclepiades of Bithynia, who utilized astrological charts to assess the health of his patients. By examining the positions of celestial bodies at the time of a patient's birth, Asclepiades was able to identify predispositions to certain illnesses, thus tailoring his medical interventions accordingly. This approach highlights the belief that the cosmos influenced physical health and that aligning treatments with astrological insights could enhance their efficacy.

Another significant example is found in the work of Galen, a prominent physician and philosopher who lived during the Hellenistic period. Galen's medical practice incorporated astrological elements, particularly in his understanding of the four humors. He believed that the alignment of planets could affect the balance of these humors within the body. In his text "On the Usefulness of the Parts of the Body," Galen elaborates on case studies where he treated patients suffering from imbalances by considering their astrological profiles. His integration of astrology into medical theory underscores the broader philosophical view that human beings are microcosms of the universe, subject to the same celestial influences.

The case of the famous philosopher and astrologer Ptolemy further exemplifies the convergence of astrology and healing. In his seminal work, the "Tetrabiblos," Ptolemy discusses the relationship between planetary movements and human health. He provides detailed accounts of how specific planetary alignments can lead to certain health conditions, guiding practitioners in their therapeutic approaches. For instance, Ptolemy noted the correlation between Saturn's placement and chronic illnesses, suggesting that treatments could be timed according to planetary transitions to optimize healing outcomes. This method reflects a sophisticated understanding of timing and celestial influence, which was pivotal in the practice of Hellenistic astrology.

The integration of astrology into therapeutic practices also had political implications. Rulers and influential figures often sought astrological guidance in making decisions about health and governance. The physician Hippocrates, revered as the father of medicine, was known to have consulted astrological advisors when addressing the health of leaders. His case studies illustrate how the health of a ruler was considered a reflection of the state itself, thus intertwining political and medical arenas. The belief that celestial events could foreshadow political turmoil or health crises reinforced the necessity of astrological insight in governance.

Lastly, the writings of ancient astrologers reveal how astrology served as a tool for healing within the context of community. Astrological practitioners would often hold public consultations, drawing on case studies of local figures to demonstrate the efficacy of their methods. This not only legitimized their practices but also fostered a sense of collective belief in astrological healing. The communal aspect of these consultations showcases the cultural importance of astrology in the Hellenistic period, where it was not merely a personal endeavor but a community-oriented practice that sought to align individual health with the greater cosmic order. Such case studies underscore the enduring legacy of Hellenistic astrology in both medical and social contexts.

Chapter 9: Notable Astrological Texts and Their Historical Contexts

The Tetrabiblos and Its Legacy

The Tetrabiblos, written by the astronomer and astrologer Claudius Ptolemy in the second century CE, stands as one of the most significant texts in the history of astrology. This foundational work systematically outlines the principles of astrological practice, integrating the knowledge of previous scholars while establishing a coherent framework for future astrologers. Ptolemy's approach combines empirical observation with theoretical reasoning, laying the groundwork for the astrological practices that would dominate both the Hellenistic world and later Western traditions. By synthesizing earlier astrological concepts, the Tetrabiblos serves as a pivotal reference point that influenced not only practitioners of astrology but also philosophical discourse within Hellenistic culture.

The legacy of the Tetrabiblos can be seen in its direct impact on the development of astrological techniques, especially regarding the use of whole sign houses and the tropical zodiac. Ptolemy's methods prioritize the relationship between celestial phenomena and terrestrial events, providing a systematic approach to interpreting astrological charts. His emphasis on the angular relationships between planets, as well as the significance of planetary dignities, shaped the methodologies utilized by later astrologers. This systematization of astrological principles helped establish a more scientific approach to astrology, distinguishing it from mere superstition and embedding it within the intellectual traditions of the time.

Moreover, the Tetrabiblos played a crucial role in connecting astrology to various aspects of ancient Greek life, including medicine and politics. Ptolemy's text discusses the influence of celestial bodies on human health and well-being, integrating astrological practices with medical theories of the time. This intersection of astrology and medicine reflects a broader Hellenistic belief in the interconnectedness of the cosmos and human existence, where astrological insights could inform medical diagnoses and treatment plans. Additionally, the application of astrology in political decision-making is evident in the text, as leaders often relied on astrological forecasts to guide their actions and policies, thereby reinforcing the practical importance of astrology in governance.

The influence of the Tetrabiblos extended beyond the Hellenistic period into Roman astrology, where its teachings were adapted and expanded by later scholars. As astrology became more integrated into Roman society, Ptolemy's work provided a foundational text that facilitated the transmission of astrological knowledge across cultures and time periods. This cross-cultural exchange enriched Roman astrological practices, leading to innovative developments while maintaining the core principles articulated in the Tetrabiblos. The text's enduring relevance is evident in its continued study and reference among astrologers throughout history, as well as its impact on the Renaissance's revival of astrological thought.

In conclusion, the Tetrabiblos remains a cornerstone of astrological literature, shaping the practices and philosophical underpinnings of astrology for centuries. Its comprehensive examination of the cosmos and its influence on earthly affairs has left an indelible mark on both the astrological community and broader cultural contexts. As astrologers continue to explore the depths of their craft, the insights and methodologies presented by Ptolemy in the Tetrabiblos serve as a vital resource, illuminating the profound connections between the stars, human experience, and the unfolding of historical events.

Other Essential Texts in Hellenistic Astrology

The exploration of Hellenistic astrology is enriched not only by its most prominent texts but also by several essential writings that contribute to our understanding of the astrological practices of the period. Among these texts, the works of key figures such as Vettius Valens, Ptolemy, and later authors like Firmicus Maternus provide critical insights into both the theoretical underpinnings and practical applications of astrology. Valens's "Anthology," for instance, offers a comprehensive compilation of astrological techniques and delineations, emphasizing the importance of personal experience and observation in astrological practice. This work is notable for its eclectic approach, integrating various astrological traditions and methodologies, which reflects the vibrant intellectual climate of the Hellenistic period.

Another significant text is Ptolemy's "Tetrabiblos," which serves as a foundational treatise on astrology. It systematically outlines the principles of astrological influence, including the relationship between celestial bodies and human affairs. Ptolemy's work is especially influential due to its systematic categorization of astrological knowledge and its attempt to align astrology with the prevailing scientific thought of the time. This text not only solidified the geocentric view of the cosmos but also provided a framework that would dominate astrological practice for centuries, influencing both Islamic and medieval European astrology.

The role of astrology in ancient Greek medicine is further illuminated by the writings of authors like Hippocrates and Galen, who integrated astrological concepts into their medical theories. The belief that celestial bodies could influence physical health and temperament was prevalent, and medical practitioners often consulted astrological charts to diagnose and treat ailments. This intersection of astrology and medicine highlights the holistic worldview of the Hellenistic period, where human health was seen as intrinsically linked to cosmic phenomena. Such texts serve as a reminder of astrology's extensive reach beyond mere prediction, embedding itself into various facets of daily life and decision-making.

The impact of Hellenistic astrology on Roman practices is evident through the adaptation of Greek texts and methods into Roman culture. Figures like Manilius and Firmicus Maternus expanded upon Hellenistic foundations, tailoring astrological practices to suit Roman societal needs. Manilius's "Astronomica" is a poetic work that weaves astrological theory with mythology, illustrating the cultural integration of astrology within the Roman literary tradition. Firmicus's "Mathesis," on the other hand, emphasizes the moral and ethical dimensions of astrology, revealing how astrological thought influenced Roman political decisions and social norms.

Lastly, the philosophical underpinnings of astrology during the Hellenistic period are articulated in the works of figures such as Plotinus and Porphyry, who sought to reconcile astrological practice with Neoplatonic thought. Their texts explore the relationship between the cosmos and the individual soul, suggesting a profound interconnectedness that underlies both astrological practice and philosophical inquiry. This synthesis of astrology and philosophy not only shaped the intellectual discourse of the time but also laid the groundwork for future developments in both fields, ensuring that the legacy of Hellenistic astrology would endure through the ages. The study of these essential texts provides a deeper understanding of the multifaceted role astrology played in shaping ancient thought and its enduring influence on subsequent traditions.

Chapter 10: The Relationship Between Philosophy and Astrology in Hellenistic Culture

Philosophical Schools and Their Views on Astrology

Philosophical schools in the Hellenistic period played a crucial role in shaping the discourse surrounding astrology, influencing its acceptance and integration into various aspects of life, from politics to medicine. The Stoics, for instance, viewed astrology as a manifestation of a deterministic universe governed by rational principles. They believed that the cosmos and human beings were interconnected, with celestial bodies exerting influence over earthly events. This perspective allowed astrology to be seen not merely as a predictive tool but as a means of understanding one's place in the universe, aligning personal actions with cosmic rhythms.

In contrast, the Epicureans adopted a more skeptical stance towards astrology, prioritizing individual agency and the randomness of the universe. They argued that while celestial phenomena could be observed, attributing specific events to planetary alignments diminished personal autonomy. This philosophical objection led to a divergence in how astrology was practiced and interpreted, with Epicureans often dismissing astrological predictions as superstitious rather than grounded in empirical observation. Despite this skepticism, some Epicureans acknowledged the practical utility of astrology in everyday life, albeit in a limited capacity.

The Neoplatonists further complicated the relationship between philosophy and astrology by introducing metaphysical elements. They posited that the cosmos was a reflection of a higher reality, with celestial bodies embodying divine intelligences. This perspective elevated astrology to a spiritual practice, where understanding the heavens became a path to accessing deeper truths about existence and the divine order. Figures like Plotinus emphasized the importance of aligning one's soul with the cosmic order, thereby integrating astrological practice into their broader metaphysical framework.

The influence of these philosophical schools extended into various practices, particularly in medicine and politics. Astrologers often collaborated with physicians, using astrological insights to diagnose ailments and prescribe remedies, a practice rooted in the belief that celestial conditions could affect health. This interdisciplinary approach underscored the legitimacy of astrology in medical contexts, as it was seen as a complementary tool alongside empirical observation. Furthermore, political leaders frequently consulted astrologers to make informed decisions, reflecting the weight that astrology held in governance during the Hellenistic period.

Ultimately, the philosophical schools of the Hellenistic era contributed to a rich tapestry of thought surrounding astrology. Each school offered distinct perspectives that shaped the understanding and application of astrological practices. The interplay between determinism, free will, metaphysical inquiry, and practical application created a complex environment where astrology could flourish. As we delve deeper into the contributions of key historical figures in Hellenistic astrology, it becomes evident that these philosophical debates were not merely academic but had profound implications for how astrology was perceived and utilized in ancient society.

Astrology's Role in Philosophical Discourse

Astrology in the Hellenistic period was not merely a system of divination; it played a pivotal role in philosophical discourse, shaping and reflecting the intellectual currents of the time. Philosophers such as Plato and Aristotle engaged with astrological concepts, exploring the implications of celestial movements on human affairs and the nature of existence itself. This synthesis of astrology and philosophy allowed for a richer understanding of the cosmos and humanity's place within it. The integration of astrological thought into philosophical frameworks provided a foundation for later philosophical inquiries, as well as for the development of astrological theories that would endure through the ages.

The alignment of astrological beliefs with philosophical inquiry often revolved around the concept of causality. Hellenistic philosophers grappled with the question of whether celestial events influence terrestrial ones or if they merely reflect a preordained cosmic order. Astrologers, drawing from the insights of philosophers, asserted that the planets and stars not only served as indicators of human fate but also as agents of change within the material world. This dialectical relationship fostered an environment where astrology could be debated, refined, and ultimately integrated into broader philosophical systems, such as Stoicism and Neoplatonism.

Moreover, the philosophical implications of astrology extended into ethical considerations, influencing how individuals perceived their actions and responsibilities. The belief in a cosmic order, where celestial bodies governed human behavior, prompted discussions on free will, destiny, and moral responsibility. Ethical philosophers examined the extent to which individuals could be held accountable for their actions if those actions were seen as predetermined by the stars. This discourse not only deepened the philosophical understanding of human agency but also provided a framework within which astrologers could position their practices as both predictive and prescriptive.

The role of astrology in political decision-making further highlights its significance in philosophical discourse. Hellenistic rulers often consulted astrologers to understand the celestial influences on their reigns, seeking guidance in matters of governance, warfare, and diplomacy. Philosophers critiqued or supported these practices, debating the legitimacy and morality of using astrology as a tool for political power. Through these discussions, astrology became intertwined with political philosophy, raising questions about the nature of authority and the ethical implications of ruling based on astrological advice.

In summary, astrology's integration into philosophical discourse during the Hellenistic period fostered a dynamic interplay that shaped both fields. The synthesis of celestial observation and philosophical inquiry enriched the understanding of human existence, ethics, and governance. As astrological practices evolved, they not only influenced individual and societal beliefs but also engaged with the philosophical questions of the time, creating a legacy that would resonate through subsequent generations. The dialogue between astrology and philosophy laid the groundwork for future astrological thought, ensuring its relevance in both intellectual and practical domains.

Chapter 11: Specific Historical Events and their Astrological Interpretations

Astrology in the Hellenistic period was not merely a tool for personal insight; it also found its application in interpreting significant historical events. The alignment of celestial bodies was often seen as a reflection of earthly happenings, with astrologers providing counsel to rulers and citizens alike. One notable event was the assassination of Julius Caesar in 44 BCE. Astrologers of the time interpreted the celestial phenomena surrounding this event, particularly the lunar eclipses and the positioning of Mars, to signify a period of turmoil and transformation for Rome. The astrological insights gleaned from these observations provided context for the political upheaval that followed, illustrating how deeply intertwined astrology was with the political landscape. Another pivotal moment for astrological interpretation was the rise of Augustus after Caesar's death. Astrologers played a crucial role in shaping public perception of Augustus as a divinely favored ruler. The prominent positioning of Jupiter in his birth chart was highlighted, suggesting prosperity and success. This astrological backing was instrumental in legitimizing his rule and establishing the new Roman Empire. The interpretations offered during this period not only influenced political decisions but also reinforced the societal belief in astrology as a guiding force in governance.

The influence of astrology can also be observed in the context of the Peloponnesian War. Astrologers provided counsel to leaders on both sides, interpreting various celestial events as omens. In particular, the conjunctions of Saturn and Jupiter were analyzed for their implications on the outcomes of battles and the fate of cities. These interpretations served to instill hope or dread among the populace, showcasing how astrological readings were utilized to shape public sentiment and decision-making during a time of great strife.

In the realm of medicine, the Hellenistic period saw a strong connection between astrology and healing practices. Events such as outbreaks of plague or significant health crises were often interpreted through an astrological lens.

Physicians would consult celestial alignments to determine the most auspicious times for treatments or surgeries. The writings of Hippocrates and Galen reflect this intertwining of astrology and medicine, emphasizing how astrological interpretations informed medical decisions and approaches to healing within the cultural context of the time.

The legacy of Hellenistic astrology extends beyond its immediate historical context, influencing subsequent astrological practices in the Roman Empire and beyond. The interpretations of key events during this period laid the groundwork for future astrological thought, as seen in the works of later figures like Ptolemy. The synthesis of astrological practices with historical events not only provided insight into the past but also shaped the future understanding of astrology's role in society. This interplay highlights the profound impact of astrology on cultural, political, and medical practices throughout the Hellenistic era and its enduring influence on subsequent traditions.

1. Fall of the Berlin Wall

Date and Time: November 9, 1989, around 10:30 p.m. (Berlin, Germany)

On November 9, 1989, around 10:30 p.m., a defining moment in history unfolded in Berlin, marking the fall of the Berlin Wall. This event not only signified the end of a significant geopolitical divide but also sparked a wave of reflection on the historical context within which such transformative events occur. For astrologers, the date and time hold particular astrological significance, as the planetary alignments can provide insights into the energies and dynamics that influenced the momentous changes in Germany and beyond. Analyzing the astrological chart for this date allows practitioners to explore how the heavens reflect human endeavors and societal shifts.

The astrological configuration on that night featured a prominent alignment of planets that resonates with themes of liberation and transformation. The transiting Uranus, known for its association with sudden change and revolutionary impulses, was in the sign of Capricorn, indicating a fundamental shift in structures of power and governance. This alignment reflects the broader societal aspirations for freedom and unity, mirroring the collective desire for change that was palpable in East Germany and throughout Eastern Europe. Astrologers can draw parallels between this alignment and historical events of uprisings and revolutions, linking the influence of Hellenistic astrology, which emphasizes the significance of planetary movements.

In the context of Hellenistic astrology, the event can be examined through the lens of whole sign houses and the tropical zodiac, both of which were foundational to the practice during ancient times. The application of these systems allows astrologers to interpret the unfolding of political events as influenced by celestial bodies. The use of the tropical zodiac, aligning the zodiac signs with the seasons, offers a perspective on how the natural cycles reflect the societal changes that occur in human life. This connection to nature and the cosmos underscores the enduring impact of Hellenistic astrological practices on modern interpretations and applications.

Moreover, the significance of the Berlin Wall's fall can be linked to the role astrology played in ancient Greek political decisions. Historically, leaders and statesmen consulted astrologers to guide their actions, shaping the course of history through celestial insights. The events of November 9 resonate with this tradition, as various movements in Eastern Europe sought validation and guidance from higher forces, paralleling the historical reliance on astrology in times of societal upheaval. The echoes of Hellenistic thought and practice in this modern context illustrate the continuity of astrological influence across time.

Finally, the interplay between astrology and philosophy in Hellenistic culture provides a rich backdrop for understanding the implications of this historical moment. The synthesis of philosophical inquiry and astrological practice formed a framework through which people sought to comprehend their reality. The fall of the Berlin Wall can be seen as a manifestation of the philosophical ideals of freedom and unity that underpin both ancient and modern societies. By examining this pivotal event through an astrological lens, astrologers can gain deeper insights into the ongoing dialogue between celestial phenomena and human experience, reaffirming the relevance of Hellenistic astrology in interpreting contemporary historical narratives.

Chart Highlights:

The Hellenistic period marked a pivotal evolution in the practice of astrology, particularly through the adoption and refinement of techniques such as whole sign houses and the tropical zodiac. These charting methods allowed astrologers to create more precise horoscopes, aligning celestial bodies with the twelve signs in a systematic way. Whole sign houses, where each sign corresponds directly to a house, simplified the interpretation process and made astrology more accessible to practitioners. This shift not only standardized the practice but also laid the groundwork for future astrological traditions, influencing both the Western and Islamic worlds.

Key historical figures such as Claudius Ptolemy and Vettius Valens were instrumental in the development of these astrological techniques. Ptolemy's work, particularly the "Tetrabiblos," synthesized earlier astrological knowledge and provided a comprehensive framework for understanding planetary movements and their implications for human affairs. Valens, on the other hand, focused on practical applications, emphasizing the importance of individual charts and their specific influences. Together, their contributions helped establish astrology as a respected field of study, integrating it deeply into the cultural and intellectual milieu of the Hellenistic era.

Astrology also played a significant role in political decision-making during the Hellenistic period. Rulers often consulted astrologers before embarking on military campaigns or making key administrative decisions. The belief that celestial alignments could predict outcomes or reveal the favor of the gods led to a close relationship between astrology and governance. This connection not only reinforced the authority of astrologers but also embedded astrological practices within the broader societal and political structures of the time.

The influence of Hellenistic astrology extended into Roman practices, where it merged with indigenous traditions to create a rich tapestry of astrological thought. Romans adopted Hellenistic techniques while also adapting them to fit their own cultural context, leading to innovations in astrological interpretation. This cross-pollination resulted in a more diverse astrological framework that would later influence medieval European astrology. The integration of these practices highlights the adaptability and resilience of astrology as it evolved through varying cultural lenses.

In the realm of medicine and healing, astrology was considered a vital tool in diagnosing and treating ailments. Ancient Greek physicians often consulted astrological charts to determine the most auspicious times for treatment or surgery, believing that celestial phenomena could influence health outcomes. This practice underscored the interconnectedness of body, mind, and cosmos in Hellenistic thought, where astrology was not just a predictive tool but a holistic approach to well-being. The insights gained from exploring notable astrological texts from this period reveal the depth of understanding that astrologers and physicians shared, ultimately shaping the foundations of both disciplines.

2. Apollo 11 Moon Landing

Date and Time: July 20, 1969, at 10:56 p.m. UTC

On July 20, 1969, at 10:56 p.m. UTC, a pivotal moment in human history occurred as Apollo 11 successfully landed on the lunar surface. This event not only marked a significant achievement in space exploration but also resonated deeply within the realms of astrology, particularly for those who engage with historical astrological contexts. The date and time of the moon landing present a unique opportunity to examine how astrological interpretations can reflect and enhance our understanding of monumental events. By analyzing the astrological chart drawn for this specific moment, astrologers can gain insights into the influences that may have shaped this historic occasion.

Astrologically, July 20, 1969, falls under the influence of the Cancer sun, a sign associated with nurturing, home, and emotions. The moon landing, a journey to the moon—a celestial body often linked to Cancerian themes—symbolizes humanity's quest for exploration and discovery. The ascendant at the time of the landing was in Aquarius, a sign that embodies innovation, progress, and a break from tradition. This combination of Cancer and Aquarius underlines the dual nature of the event, representing both the emotional significance of reaching a new frontier and the intellectual drive for advancement that characterized the 1960s.

In the context of Hellenistic astrology, the principles of Whole Sign Houses and the Tropical Zodiac can provide a framework for understanding the implications of this event. The placement of planets within the chart can reveal the underlying currents that influenced not only the moon landing but also the societal context surrounding it. For instance, the conjunction of the moon with the nodes in the chart may suggest a collective karmic moment, indicating that this achievement was not merely an individual accomplishment but a reflection of humanity's shared aspirations and struggles. Hellenistic astrologers recognized the importance of planetary alignments and their potential to influence earthly matters, a perspective that remains relevant in contemporary astrological practices.

The influence of the Hellenistic period on astrology practices is particularly notable when considering the philosophical underpinnings that shaped astrological thought. The synthesis of astrology with philosophical inquiry during this era laid the foundation for understanding the interconnectedness of cosmic events and human affairs. The moon landing can thus be seen as an embodiment of these Hellenistic ideals, where the pursuit of knowledge and exploration aligns with a deeper philosophical quest for meaning in the universe. Astrologers can draw parallels between the aspirations of ancient Greek thinkers and the modern quest for understanding our place in the cosmos, reinforcing the idea that astrology serves as a bridge between the celestial and the terrestrial.

Moreover, the role of astrology in ancient Greek political decisions offers a critical lens through which to view the moon landing. Historically, astrological insights were often consulted to guide leaders and nations in their pursuits. The Apollo 11 mission, undertaken during a time of significant political tension and competition, can be interpreted as a manifestation of collective ambition and determination. Understanding the astrological context of this event allows astrologers to appreciate how historical figures may have harnessed celestial influences to guide their decisions, reflecting patterns that resonate through time. This connection to Hellenistic traditions underscores the enduring relevance of astrology in shaping human endeavors, from the political to the exploratory.

Chart Highlights:

The Hellenistic period marks a transformative era in the evolution of astrology, characterized by the integration of Babylonian, Egyptian, and Greek astronomical knowledge. This fusion laid the groundwork for the sophisticated astrological practices that would define Western astrology. The use of whole sign houses became popular during this time, simplifying the interpretation of charts by assigning each house to an entire sign, thus enhancing the accessibility and accuracy of readings. This method contrasts sharply with the earlier quadrant systems, emphasizing the importance of sign placement over angular distance, which allowed practitioners to focus more on the symbolic meanings of signs rather than complex mathematical calculations.

The tropical zodiac also emerged as a significant development within Hellenistic astrology, establishing a framework that aligned astrological practices with the seasons rather than the fixed stars. This shift reflected a deeper philosophical understanding of the relationship between cosmic phenomena and terrestrial events. The tropical zodiac's emphasis on the equinoxes and solstices connected astrology more closely with agricultural cycles, reinforcing its relevance in guiding decisions related to farming and seasonal activities. As a result, astrologers began to view their work not just as a means of divination but as a tool for understanding and navigating the natural world.

Key historical figures such as Ptolemy, Vettius Valens, and Firmicus Maternus made substantial contributions to the body of astrological knowledge during the Hellenistic period. Ptolemy's "Tetrabiblos" synthesized existing astrological wisdom and established foundational principles that influenced both contemporary and later practitioners. Valens's "Anthology" provided a wealth of practical techniques and insights, showcasing the application of astrology in everyday life. Firmicus Maternus brought forth a more philosophical approach, exploring the moral implications of astrological practice. Together, these figures not only advanced technical understanding but also shaped the ethical and philosophical discourse surrounding astrology. Astrology's role in ancient Greek political decisions underscores its significance beyond personal guidance. Leaders and statesmen frequently consulted astrologers to gain insights into favorable timings for military campaigns, public announcements, and other critical events. This reliance on astrological counsel illustrates the deep interconnection between celestial observations and political authority during the Hellenistic period. The belief that the cosmos influenced human affairs lent legitimacy to rulers and their decisions, demonstrating how astrology served as a vital tool for governance and social order.

The influence of Hellenistic astrology extended into Roman practices, where it continued to evolve and adapt to new cultural contexts. Roman astrologers adopted and modified Hellenistic techniques, integrating them into their own systems of thought, which included a growing interest in personal horoscopes and individual destiny. Moreover, the impact of Hellenistic astrology on medicine and healing practices cannot be overlooked. Physicians often utilized astrological charts to determine the most auspicious times for treatments, reflecting a holistic view of health that intertwined spiritual and physical well-being. The legacy of this period is evident in the continued relevance of astrological texts and practices, which have shaped not only the history of astrology but also its integration into various aspects of life throughout the ages.

3. Signing of the Declaration of Independence

Date and Time: July 4, 1776, around 2 p.m. (Philadelphia, Pennsylvania)

On July 4, 1776, around 2 p.m., the atmosphere in Philadelphia was charged with a sense of revolutionary fervor. This moment marked not only the adoption of the Declaration of Independence but also a significant shift in the political landscape of the American colonies. Astrologers examining this pivotal date must consider the celestial configurations that accompanied such a monumental event. The alignment of planets, particularly in relation to the angles of the chart, can offer insights into the motivations and prospects of the nascent nation, reflecting the strong influence of Hellenistic astrological practices that were well-established by that time.

The use of the Tropical Zodiac, which aligns with the seasons, plays a crucial role in interpreting the astrological implications of this date. The Sun was in Cancer, symbolizing themes of home, family, and emotional security. This positioning resonates with the colonists' desire for autonomy and their yearning to establish a government that reflected their values. Astrologers can analyze how the prominence of Cancer in the chart correlates with the foundational principles of the Declaration, emphasizing the importance of life, liberty, and the pursuit of happiness. This zodiacal sign may also suggest an underlying protective instinct, indicative of the colonies' determination to guard their rights against perceived tyranny.

Hellenistic astrology's influence on the political decisions of the time is evident when considering the aspects between key planetary positions. The conjunctions and oppositions present in the chart reveal tensions and synergies that likely informed the leaders' decision-making processes. For instance, any significant aspects involving Mars and Saturn could indicate the struggle between the desire for independence and the discipline required to achieve it. These astrological factors highlight how ancient practices informed contemporary political actions, suggesting that the Founding Fathers may have been guided, whether consciously or unconsciously, by astrological principles that had been handed down through generations.

The connection between astrology and medicine during the Hellenistic period also merits consideration when discussing the health of the emerging nation. Astrologers of the time often used celestial events to diagnose and treat ailments. The presence of particular planets in the chart could signify the collective health of the population, both physically and politically. Analyzing the astrological chart for July 4, 1776, could reveal insights into the societal conditions of the colonies, possibly indicating periods of turmoil or stability that would influence the well-being of the populace. This relationship underscores the multifaceted role astrology played in Hellenistic culture, extending beyond mere prediction into realms of governance and public welfare.

Finally, the philosophical underpinnings of astrology during the Hellenistic era shaped the worldview of the revolutionaries. The blending of astrological thought with philosophical inquiry fostered a deeper understanding of the cosmos and humanity's place within it. The principles articulated by key figures in Hellenistic astrology, such as Ptolemy, emphasized the interconnectedness of celestial movements and earthly events. By examining the astrological chart of July 4, 1776, one can discern how these philosophical ideas may have influenced the Founding Fathers' perspectives on destiny and free will, thus enriching the narrative of a nation striving to define its identity in the face of monumental change.

Chart Highlights:

The Hellenistic period marked a significant evolution in astrological practices, where the integration of philosophical thought and empirical observation transformed astrology into a more systematic and respected discipline. Key figures such as Claudius Ptolemy and Vettius Valens contributed substantially to the corpus of astrological knowledge during this era. Their works, notably the Tetrabiblos and the Anthology, not only codified existing astrological techniques but also introduced innovative concepts such as the use of whole sign houses and the application of the tropical zodiac. These developments laid the groundwork for subsequent astrological practices and shaped the trajectory of astrology in both the Western and Roman contexts.

One of the most notable features of Hellenistic astrology was its emphasis on the relationship between celestial phenomena and terrestrial events, particularly in the realm of political decision-making. Astrologers were often consulted by rulers and statesmen, who sought to align their policies with the perceived cosmic order. The astrological charts created for significant political events, such as battles or royal ascensions, were believed to reveal insights into the outcomes of these actions. This integration of astrology into governance not only underscored its importance in ancient society but also reflected the belief in a divine order that permeated both the cosmos and human affairs.

The medical practices of the Hellenistic period also showcased the interplay between astrology and healing. Physicians like Hippocrates and Galen recognized the influence of celestial bodies on human health, leading to the development of astrological medicine. Treatments were often tailored to align with specific planetary positions, emphasizing the interconnectedness of body and cosmos. This practice not only informed medical diagnoses but also illustrated how prevalent astrological thought was in everyday life, influencing not just the elite but also the general populace who sought healing and understanding through these astrological insights.

The impact of Hellenistic astrology on Roman practices cannot be overstated. As Rome absorbed Greek culture, the astrological traditions of the Hellenistic period were adapted and integrated into Roman society. This resulted in the development of unique Roman interpretations of astrology, where astrological elements merged with local beliefs and practices. The Roman adaptation of astrology emphasized personal horoscopy and the use of detailed natal charts, further popularizing astrology among the elite and common citizens alike. The writings of later Roman astrologers demonstrated the enduring legacy of Hellenistic thought, showcasing how these ancient practices continued to evolve and resonate through time.

Astrology in the Hellenistic era was not merely a tool for prediction but also a profound philosophical system intertwined with ethics, metaphysics, and the nature of existence. The philosophical underpinnings of astrology during this period, particularly the works of thinkers like Plotinus and the Neoplatonists, fostered a deeper understanding of the cosmos as a living entity, influencing both astrological interpretation and practice. This relationship between philosophy and astrology enriched the intellectual landscape of the time, allowing for a more nuanced approach to astrological study that emphasized not only the mechanics of celestial movements but also their significance in the broader tapestry of human experience and the pursuit of knowledge.

4. End of World War II (V-E Day)

Date and Time: May 8, 1945, around 3 p.m. UTC

On May 8, 1945, at approximately 3 p.m. UTC, a significant moment in history unfolded, marking the end of World War II in Europe. The astrological implications of this date resonate deeply within the context of Western Hellenistic astrology, particularly as it relates to the understanding of global events and their alignment with celestial phenomena. Astrologers often look to historic dates to derive insights and patterns that may inform contemporary practices. Analyzing the positions of celestial bodies at this moment can reveal insights into the collective psyche of humanity and highlight the astrological signatures that accompany major shifts in political landscapes.

The sky on this date featured a prominent configuration that included the Moon in Libra, which suggests themes of balance, diplomacy, and the restoration of peace. Libra, ruled by Venus, emphasizes relationships and harmony, making it particularly meaningful that a moment celebrated for ending conflict was marked by a sign associated with reconciliation. Astrologers may interpret this lunar position as indicative of a collective desire for unity and stability following years of turmoil. The conjunction of the Moon with the North Node further underscores the potential for new beginnings, hinting at a karmic resolution that could guide the future of European nations. Additionally, the Sun in Taurus at this time highlights themes of security and material stability, traits that resonate with the post-war recovery efforts that would soon follow. Taurus, an earth sign, represents the practical steps necessary for rebuilding and re-establishing a sense of normalcy. As the Sun moved through this sign, the collective focus shifted toward tangible resources and the importance of nurturing the land and economy. For astrologers, this placement could suggest that the efforts to heal and renew would be rooted in practical, grounded approaches, aligning well with the historical context of rebuilding war-torn nations.

The influence of Hellenistic astrological practices is evident not only in the analysis of specific planetary configurations but also in the collective consciousness of the time. The astrological traditions that emerged during the Hellenistic period laid the groundwork for how future generations of astrologers interpret significant historical events. By employing techniques such as whole sign houses and the tropical zodiac, practitioners can derive meaning from celestial events in ways that reflect the philosophies and methodologies established by key historical figures in astrology. Their contributions continue to shape the dialogue around the role of astrology in political and social decision-making.

In conclusion, the astrological significance of May 8, 1945, serves as a reminder of the enduring relevance of Hellenistic astrology in understanding pivotal moments in history. The interplay of celestial bodies at this time not only encapsulates themes of resolution and rebirth but also connects to the broader narrative of how astrology has influenced human affairs across cultures and epochs. As astrologers examine this date, they can draw upon the rich traditions of Hellenistic practices to gain insights into the complexities of political landscapes and the healing processes that follow profound societal upheaval.

Chart Highlights:

The Hellenistic period marked a significant evolution in astrological practices, characterized by the development of whole sign houses and the adoption of the tropical zodiac. These innovations shifted the focus from the previous methods of astrology that were predominantly concerned with planetary positions relative to fixed stars. The chart highlights from this era illustrate how these systems provided a more structured approach to interpreting natal charts. Whole sign houses allowed astrologers to assign entire signs to houses, simplifying calculations and enhancing interpretive clarity. This method gained popularity because it aligned with the philosophical underpinnings of the time, emphasizing a more direct relationship between celestial movements and earthly events.

Key historical figures such as Ptolemy, Vettius Valens, and Firmicus Maternus played pivotal roles in shaping astrological thought during the Hellenistic period. Their writings encapsulated the theoretical advancements and practical applications of astrology. For instance, Ptolemy's "Tetrabiblos" synthesized earlier astrological traditions and introduced concepts that would dominate medieval astrology. The contributions of these figures are evident in their charts, which not only display their innovative techniques but also reflect the sociopolitical contexts in which they operated, intertwining astrology with the prevailing philosophical and scientific ideas of their time.

The integration of astrology into political decision-making was another hallmark of the Hellenistic period. Rulers often consulted astrologers to guide their actions, reflecting the belief that celestial phenomena could influence earthly affairs. The charts from this period often reveal the interplay between astrological predictions and significant political events, such as the rise and fall of dynasties. Astrologers wielded considerable influence, as their interpretations could sway public opinion and authenticate political legitimacy. This practice highlighted the essential role of astrology not only in personal guidance but also in the broader governance of society.

Hellenistic astrology also laid the groundwork for its later adoption and adaptation by Roman practitioners. The Roman period saw a fusion of Greek astrological techniques with local traditions, further expanding the scope and application of astrology. Charts from this transitional phase demonstrate how Roman astrologers incorporated elements from Hellenistic practices while developing their unique interpretations. This evolution facilitated the spread of astrology across the Roman Empire, making it an integral part of both public life and personal belief systems, thereby perpetuating its significance across cultures.

The use of astrology in ancient Greek medicine is another crucial area where chart highlights reveal the interplay between celestial observations and health practices. Medical practitioners employed astrological insights to determine the best times for treatments, aligning their practices with cosmic cycles. The charts from this intersection of medicine and astrology demonstrate how healers considered planetary positions to be indicative of bodily conditions and potential recovery. This holistic approach to health, rooted in astrological principles, underscores the integral role of astrology in various facets of Hellenistic life, showcasing its enduring legacy in both personal and communal contexts.

5. Fall of Constantinople

Date and Time: May 29, 1453, around sunrise (Istanbul, Turkey)

On May 29, 1453, around sunrise, the city of Constantinople, known today as Istanbul, experienced a momentous event that would reshape the political landscape of both the East and West. The fall of Constantinople to the Ottoman Empire marked the end of the Byzantine Empire, an event that not only shifted territorial boundaries but also influenced the astrological practices of the time. Astrologers of the Hellenistic tradition were acutely aware of the celestial configurations that accompanied significant historical moments, and this particular date serves as a pivotal case study in understanding the interplay between astrology and historical events. Astrologically, the conditions surrounding the fall of Constantinople can be analyzed through the lens of the whole sign houses and the tropical zodiac, which were prevalent in Hellenistic astrology. The rising sign at sunrise on that fateful day was critical in determining the astrological influences at play. The positions of the planets and their aspects would have been scrutinized by astrologers seeking to interpret the implications of the event not only for the city but for the broader Mediterranean world. Such analysis provides insight into how astrologers utilized celestial movements to forecast political outcomes, revealing the deeply intertwined nature of astrology and governance in the Hellenistic tradition.

Key historical figures in Hellenistic astrology, such as Ptolemy and Valens, had long established frameworks for interpreting significant events through astrological lenses. Their contributions laid the groundwork for understanding how the planetary configurations on the day of the siege could be interpreted. Astrologers of the time would have referenced texts and methodologies from these influential figures to assess the potential ramifications of the fall of Constantinople, thereby placing the event within a larger astrological narrative that transcended regional politics and connected to universal principles.

The role of astrology in ancient Greek political decisions cannot be overstated, as leaders often consulted astrologers to gauge the suitability of actions based on celestial alignments. The fall of Constantinople represents a culmination of astrological predictions and political maneuvers that had been in the making for decades. This event not only illustrated the practical applications of astrology in statecraft but also highlighted the cultural transition from a Hellenistic worldview to one influenced by Islamic astrology, as the Ottomans embraced the astrological traditions that had developed in the region.

The impact of Hellenistic astrology on Roman practices further underscores the significance of this date. As the Ottoman Empire rose to power, it inherited a rich astrological tradition that had been shaped by both Greek and Roman influences. The fall of Constantinople, as a historical marker, can thus be viewed as a turning point in the evolution of astrological thought, linking the ancient practices of the Hellenistic period with the burgeoning astrological frameworks that would eventually spread throughout Europe. This transition not only affected political and military strategies but also had profound implications for the fields of medicine, healing, and philosophy, reinforcing the enduring legacy of Hellenistic astrology in shaping the worldview of subsequent generations.

Chart Highlights:

The Hellenistic period marked a significant evolution in the practice of astrology, characterized by the establishment of whole sign houses and the adaptation of the tropical zodiac. This era saw the integration of various astrological traditions, culminating in a cohesive system that influenced both practitioners and scholars. Whole sign houses, where each house is defined by an entire sign of the zodiac, simplified the interpretation process and made astrology more accessible to a broader audience. This approach allowed astrologers to convey complex astrological concepts with greater clarity, enhancing the practice's appeal and functionality.

Key historical figures emerged during this period, each contributing unique insights and techniques that shaped Hellenistic astrology. Prominent figures such as Ptolemy and Vettius Valens are often highlighted for their foundational texts that explored the intricacies of astrological practice. Ptolemy's "Tetrabiblos" provided a comprehensive framework for understanding astrology's role within the cosmos, while Valens' "Anthology" offered practical applications of astrological theory. These works not only preserved earlier knowledge but also introduced innovative ideas that would resonate through subsequent generations of astrologers.

Astrology's role in ancient Greek political decisions exemplifies its integration into the fabric of Hellenistic society. Leaders often sought astrological guidance to inform their strategic choices, believing that celestial patterns could influence earthly outcomes. The decisions made during this period, whether related to warfare, governance, or public policy, were frequently intertwined with astrological counsel, highlighting astrology's perceived authority in shaping historical events. This relationship between astrology and politics not only legitimized astrological practices but also reinforced its status as a crucial component of statecraft.

The influence of Hellenistic astrology extended into Roman practices, where it underwent further adaptation and integration into a broader cultural context. Roman astrologers built upon Hellenistic traditions, incorporating elements that resonated with their own societal values and beliefs. This cross-cultural exchange enriched astrological practices and texts, resulting in a vibrant tradition that influenced various aspects of Roman life, including medicine, philosophy, and governance. The synthesis of Hellenistic and Roman astrological thought laid the groundwork for future developments in astrology across Europe.

Astrology also played a pivotal role in ancient Greek medicine and healing practices, with physicians often employing astrological insights to diagnose and treat ailments. The correspondence between celestial phenomena and human health was a prevailing belief, leading to a holistic approach that considered the individual's astrological chart as a vital tool in understanding their physical and psychological well-being. Notable texts, such as those by Hippocrates and Galen, reflect this interconnection, illustrating how astrology informed medical practices and contributed to the overall understanding of health within the Hellenistic framework. The interplay between astrology and medicine reveals the depth of Hellenistic thought and its lasting impact on various domains of knowledge.

6. Assassination of Archduke Franz Ferdinand

Date and Time: June 28, 1914, at 10:45 a.m. (Sarajevo, Bosnia)

On June 28, 1914, at 10:45 a.m., Sarajevo became the backdrop for an event that would reshape the course of history. This moment marked the assassination of Archduke Franz Ferdinand of Austria and his wife, Sophie, which triggered a cascade of geopolitical tensions leading to World War I. For astrologers examining this date, the astrological chart reveals significant alignments that speak to the broader implications of this event within the context of Hellenistic astrology. The positioning of planets at that moment provides insight into both personal and collective destinies, illustrating how astrology can reflect the tumultuous nature of human affairs.

Astrologically, the chart for this fateful moment shows a prominent presence of Mars, the planet traditionally associated with conflict and aggression, in a challenging aspect with Saturn, symbolizing authority and structure. This configuration hints at the underlying tensions between established powers and emerging nationalistic fervor, a theme prevalent in the Balkans during this period. The opposition between Mars and Saturn may also reflect the sense of inevitability that accompanied the assassination—a clash between the desires of the individual and the rigidity of political systems. Such astrological insights can help modern astrologers understand how the dynamics of power and conflict were written in the stars even before the events unfolded.

In the context of the Hellenistic astrological tradition, the use of whole sign houses emphasizes the importance of the ascendant and its lord in interpreting the unfolding of significant events. The ascendant of the Sarajevo chart, positioned in a cardinal sign, points to a moment ripe with potential for action and change, aligning with the historical context of rising tensions in Europe. The cardinal modality reflects initiatory energy, suggesting that the assassination was not just a singular act of violence but a catalyst for broader societal shifts, illuminating the interconnectedness of individual actions and collective outcomes.

Moreover, the influence of Hellenistic astrology on the practices of subsequent cultures is apparent in the way astrological interpretations have evolved to incorporate historical events. The assassination of Franz Ferdinand can be seen as a pivotal moment, not only in astrology but also in political decision-making. The alignments present in the chart invite astrologers to consider how celestial influences were understood and utilized by political figures in the past, paralleling the way astrology continues to inform contemporary political analysis. This historical reflection is critical as it connects the past with the present, showcasing the enduring relevance of astrological insights in navigating complex social landscapes.

Lastly, the relationship between astrology and philosophy in Hellenistic culture provides a rich context for interpreting the events of June 28, 1914. The philosophical underpinnings of astrology during the Hellenistic period emphasized the interconnectedness of the cosmos and human affairs, suggesting that each event, including the assassination, has implications that reverberate through time. For astrologers today, this perspective encourages a holistic understanding of historical events, recognizing that the lessons learned from the past can inform both personal and collective approaches to the future. The significance of this date lies not only in its historical impact but also in its astrological resonance, reminding us of the timeless interplay between celestial movements and human destiny.

Chart Highlights:

The Hellenistic period marked a significant evolution in astrological practices, particularly through the adoption and refinement of whole sign houses and the tropical zodiac. Whole sign houses simplified the astrological framework, allowing practitioners to interpret charts based on entire signs rather than divisions within them. This method not only contributed to a more intuitive understanding of planetary positions but also eased the complexities associated with the earlier systems of house division. The tropical zodiac further established a connection between celestial phenomena and earthly seasons, underscoring the belief that cosmic events could influence human affairs. These innovations laid the groundwork for future astrological practices that would endure well into the Roman era and beyond.

Key historical figures emerged during the Hellenistic period, each contributing unique insights and methodologies to astrology. Figures such as Ptolemy, who compiled essential astrological texts, synthesized earlier knowledge and introduced rigorous empirical methods. His work, the Tetrabiblos, served as a cornerstone for astrology, establishing principles that would influence both contemporaries and future generations of astrologers. Similarly, other scholars like Vettius Valens and Paulus Alexandrinus provided practical applications of astrological theory, emphasizing the importance of individualized chart interpretation. Their contributions not only enriched the astrological tradition but also highlighted the collaborative nature of knowledge during this dynamic era.

Astrology played a crucial role in the political landscape of ancient Greece, influencing decisions and strategies among leaders and states. The practice was often employed to time significant events, such as military campaigns or the founding of colonies, based on auspicious planetary alignments. Rulers sought astrological counsel to determine the most favorable moments for action, believing that cosmic forces could sway outcomes in their favor. This reliance on astrology for political decisions illustrates the profound impact of celestial observations on governance and societal structures, revealing a culture that intertwined the heavens with earthly power dynamics.

The transition from Hellenistic to Roman practices saw a further integration of astrology into everyday life and governance. Roman leaders adopted and adapted Hellenistic techniques, creating a unique blend that incorporated local traditions and beliefs. This period witnessed the emergence of personal horoscopes, allowing individuals to seek guidance based on their unique celestial configurations. The influence of Hellenistic astrologers remained evident as their texts continued to circulate, shaping Roman interpretations of astrology and expanding its application across various aspects of life, from politics to personal decisions.

Astrology's intersection with medicine in ancient Greece highlights its integral role in holistic healing practices. Physicians often consulted celestial charts to diagnose ailments and determine appropriate treatments, illustrating the belief that human health was closely linked to cosmic influences. Notable texts, such as those by Hippocrates, acknowledged the relevance of astrological factors in medical contexts, suggesting that practitioners of the time recognized the importance of aligning therapeutic approaches with the rhythms of the universe. This fusion of astrology and medicine not only enriched both fields but also underscored the multifaceted nature of Hellenistic thought, where philosophy, science, and spirituality converged in a quest for understanding the human condition.

7. Great Fire of London

Date and Time: September 2, 1666, around 1 a.m. (London, England)

The date and time of September 2, 1666, around 1 a.m. in London, England, marks a significant moment in the annals of both astrological history and the broader context of societal upheaval. This period was characterized by the aftermath of the Great Fire of London, which had devastated much of the city just weeks prior. Astrologers of the time were keenly aware of the celestial movements and their implications on earthly events. The alignment of planets during this hour held a deeper significance, connecting the tumultuous earthly events to the divine influences of the cosmos, reflecting the ongoing dialogue between the terrestrial and celestial realms that was central to Hellenistic astrological practices.

Astrology, rooted in the Hellenistic tradition, leveraged the principles of Whole Sign Houses and the Tropical Zodiac, both of which were pivotal in interpreting the astrological chart of this moment. The configurations of planets in relation to fixed stars and the zodiac signs would have been meticulously analyzed by contemporary astrologers. They understood that the positions and aspects of celestial bodies could offer insights into not only personal destinies but also the fate of the state itself. The astrological community sought to interpret the implications of the Great Fire, using these traditional frameworks to predict future events and guide political decisions.

The influence of the Hellenistic period on astrology practices, particularly during the 17th century, cannot be overstated. Astrologers drew upon ancient texts and integrated Hellenistic methodologies with emerging practices. Figures such as William Lilly exemplified the synthesis of these ancient teachings with modern contexts, as they sought to apply astrological principles to contemporary issues, including the recovery and rebuilding of London post-fire. This blending of historical and practical applications of astrology highlighted the continuity of astrological thought from the Hellenistic era through to early modern Europe.

Astrology's role in political decisions during this time was profoundly significant. Political leaders and decision-makers often consulted astrologers to understand the implications of celestial events on governance and public policy. The fire in London served as a catalyst for reflection on the moral and spiritual state of the city, leading to inquiries into whether the disaster was a sign of divine displeasure or a call for reform. The astrological interpretations of this event played a crucial role in shaping public sentiment and guiding political action in the wake of the calamity.

Furthermore, the impact of Hellenistic astrology on Roman practices is evident in the continued emphasis on the relationship between celestial phenomena and human affairs. The methodologies developed during the Hellenistic period provided a foundation for subsequent astrological practices in Europe, especially in how medicine and healing were approached. Astrologers utilized charts not only to predict societal outcomes but also to inform medical treatments, believing in the interconnectedness of body, mind, and cosmos. The astrological chart cast for the early morning of September 2, 1666, can thus be seen as a reflection of these deep-seated beliefs, encapsulating a moment where the legacy of Hellenistic astrology continued to exert influence over various aspects of life, even in a rapidly changing world.

Chart Highlights:

The study of Hellenistic astrology is enriched by the examination of various charts that exemplify the methodologies and principles of this ancient practice. Notably, the use of Whole Sign Houses marks a significant departure from the more complex system of quadrant houses that emerged later. Whole Sign Houses assign each sign of the zodiac to an entire house, simplifying the interpretation process. This charting technique not only enhances clarity but also aligns with the philosophical underpinnings of Hellenistic thought, where the cosmos is viewed as an integrated whole. The charts from this period highlight the emphasis on planetary rulerships and their direct influence on personal and political destinies, offering insights into the astrological practices that shaped the era.

Examining the charts from key historical events reveals the profound impact of Hellenistic astrology on political decisions in ancient Greece. Astrologers of this time often provided counsel to rulers, interpreting celestial phenomena to guide military campaigns and governance. For instance, charts drawn for significant battles or political shifts showcase the astrological alignments that were believed to forecast success or failure. The role of astrology as a tool for decision-making underscores its integration into the fabric of Hellenistic society, where the movements of the heavens were seen as direct reflections of earthly affairs.

The contributions of prominent figures such as Ptolemy and Hipparchus are essential in understanding the evolution of Hellenistic astrology. Their works, which are often represented in charts that illustrate their methodologies, serve as foundational texts for subsequent generations. Ptolemy's "Tetrabiblos," with its systematic approach to astrology, is particularly notable for its blend of empirical observation and theoretical framework. Charts derived from their teachings reveal the intricate relationships between planets, signs, and houses, providing a rich context for practitioners looking to harness the wisdom of their predecessors.

The intersection of astrology and medicine during the Hellenistic period is another area of significant exploration, as illustrated by various medical astrology charts. These charts emphasize the belief that celestial bodies influence health and disease, with specific planetary alignments linked to particular ailments. Practitioners utilized astrological insights to tailor treatments, demonstrating the holistic approach of Hellenistic physicians who integrated astrological knowledge into their medical practices. This relationship between astrology and healing not only reflects the cultural significance of astrology but also its practical applications in everyday life.

Finally, the philosophical dimensions of Hellenistic astrology can be observed in the charts that illustrate the connections between cosmic phenomena and human experience. The philosophical schools of thought, such as Stoicism and Neoplatonism, deeply influenced astrological interpretation during this period. Charts that align astrological events with philosophical ideas reveal a worldview where the cosmos and human affairs are intertwined. This synthesis of astrology and philosophy highlights the intellectual rigor of Hellenistic astrologers, who sought to understand the divine order of the universe and its implications for human existence.

8. Women's Suffrage Granted in the U.S.

Date and Time: August 18, 1920 (noon, Nashville, Tennessee)

On August 18, 1920, at noon in Nashville, Tennessee, a significant astrological moment unfolded, resonating with the echoes of ancient Hellenistic practices. This date marks a pivotal point in the evolution of astrology as it intersects with contemporary events. Astrologers recognize this moment as a time when the influences of the cosmos can be analyzed through the lens of Hellenistic traditions, particularly the use of whole sign houses and the tropical zodiac. The alignment of celestial bodies on this date provides a rich tapestry for examining how Hellenistic astrology continues to shape modern interpretations and applications.

The position of the planets on this date reflects the enduring legacy of key historical figures within the Hellenistic astrological tradition. Astrologers from the Hellenistic period laid the groundwork for techniques that are still in use today, such as the calculation of planetary aspects and the interpretation of transits. The astrological chart for this specific moment serves as a reminder of how these ancient methodologies have been preserved and adapted over time. By analyzing the chart, astrologers can gain insights into the influences that were at play during the early 20th century, a time marked by social and political upheaval.

As the Hellenistic period was characterized by the integration of astrology into political decision-making, the astrological patterns from August 18, 1920, can also be contextualized within the framework of political astrology. The aftermath of World War I and the subsequent societal changes in the United States provide a compelling backdrop for understanding the astrological influences at play. The chart can be examined for indicators of shifts in public sentiment, legislative changes, and the broader cultural movements that were emerging during this time.

The impact of Hellenistic astrology on Roman practices also plays a significant role in understanding the astrological environment of the early 20th century. The blending of Greek and Roman astrological traditions led to the refinement of astrological techniques that would later influence Western astrology. By exploring the astrological implications of the Nashville chart in this context, astrologers can trace a lineage of thought that connects ancient practices to modern interpretations, highlighting the continuity of astrological wisdom through the ages.

Finally, the relationship between astrology and philosophy in Hellenistic culture is crucial to understanding the significance of the August 18, 1920, chart. This date encapsulates a moment where philosophical inquiries into the nature of the cosmos intersect with astrological practice, reflecting a broader human desire to decipher the universe's influence on earthly affairs. The astrological analysis of this date not only reveals the specific planetary positions but also prompts deeper reflections on the philosophical underpinnings that have shaped astrological thought throughout history.

Chart Highlights:

In the realm of Hellenistic astrology, the significance of chart interpretation cannot be overstated. The practice of using whole sign houses, a defining feature of Hellenistic techniques, allows astrologers to see the entire zodiac as a coherent narrative, wherein each house corresponds directly to a sign. This method contrasts sharply with the later quadrant systems and offers a unique lens through which to analyze personal and collective destinies. The emphasis on whole sign houses not only simplifies the interpretation process but also reinforces the interconnectedness of astrological elements, providing a holistic perspective that resonates deeply with the philosophical traditions of the time. The Hellenistic period marked a transformative era for astrology, as it absorbed and synthesized various influences from Babylonian and Egyptian practices. This cross-cultural exchange enriched astrological methodology and led to the formalization of key concepts such as the zodiacal signs and planetary dignities. The introduction of the tropical zodiac, which aligns the signs with the seasons, further adapted astrology to the Mediterranean context. This adaptation not only made astrology more relevant to the lives of practitioners but also laid the groundwork for its future evolution in Roman culture and beyond, demonstrating the dynamic nature of astrological practices during this period.

Key historical figures such as Ptolemy and Vettius Valens made significant contributions to the field of astrology during the Hellenistic age. Ptolemy's "Tetrabiblos" serves as a foundational text, harmonizing astronomical observations with astrological principles. Valens, on the other hand, emphasized the importance of personal horoscopes and the analysis of individual life events, showcasing the diverse approaches within Hellenistic astrology. Their works not only preserved astrological knowledge but also influenced subsequent generations of astrologers, creating a lineage of thought that continues to shape modern practices. The rich tapestry of ideas from these figures highlights the intellectual rigor present in Hellenistic astrology.

Astrology played a pivotal role in ancient Greek political decisions, serving as both a tool for guidance and a means of legitimizing authority. Leaders often consulted astrologers to determine auspicious times for significant actions, such as battles or public gatherings. This reliance on astrological insight underscores the belief in a cosmic order that governed earthly affairs, intertwining the fates of individuals with broader societal outcomes. The intertwining of astrology with politics not only reflects the cultural values of the time but also illustrates how astrology functioned as an integral part of decision-making processes.

The impact of Hellenistic astrology on Roman practices cannot be overlooked, as it provided the foundation for the astrological traditions that flourished in the Roman Empire. Roman astrologers adopted and adapted Hellenistic techniques, further evolving the practice to meet the needs of a diverse population. Additionally, the use of astrology in ancient Greek medicine and healing practices highlights its multifaceted role in society, as practitioners sought to align physical health with celestial movements. Notable astrological texts from this era, coupled with the philosophical underpinnings of Hellenistic thought, reveal a culture deeply engaged with the cosmos, where astrology served as a bridge between the heavens and human experience.

9. French Revolution Begins

Date and Time: May 5, 1789, around 9 a.m. (Versailles, France)

On May 5, 1789, at approximately 9 a.m., Versailles became a focal point not only for political upheaval but also for astrological significance. This date marked the convening of the Estates-General, a critical event leading to the French Revolution. Astrologers examining this moment can glean insights based on the planetary alignments and configurations present at the time, reflecting the tensions and transformations that would soon engulf France. The positioning of celestial bodies, particularly the Moon and its aspects, can be analyzed to understand the emotional climate and public sentiment surrounding this pivotal gathering.

The chart for this date reveals significant astrological features that resonate with the themes of revolution and change. The presence of Uranus, a planet associated with upheaval and innovation, in a prominent position suggests an atmosphere ripe for radical ideas. This echoes the Enlightenment ideals that had been permeating French society, advocating for liberty, equality, and fraternity. Astrologers can interpret these celestial dynamics as indicators of societal shifts, emphasizing how astrology can illuminate the motivations behind historical events.

Furthermore, the influence of the Hellenistic tradition can be traced in the astrological practices of the time. The use of Whole Sign Houses and the Tropical Zodiac, both rooted in Hellenistic astrology, provided a framework for analyzing political and social phenomena. This approach allows astrologers to assess the implications of the planetary positions in relation to the houses that govern various aspects of life, including governance, public affairs, and collective consciousness. The relevance of Hellenistic astrological principles in the context of 1789 underscores the continuity and evolution of astrological thought through the centuries.

In the realm of political decisions, astrology had long played a role in shaping leadership and governance. Historical figures often consulted astrologers to discern auspicious timings for significant actions. The convening of the Estates-

General was not merely a political maneuver; it was steeped in astrological considerations that reflected the leaders' attempts to navigate the turbulent waters of public sentiment and political power. The astrological context of May 5, 1789, thus serves as a reminder of the intertwined nature of astrology and politics throughout history.

Finally, the examination of this date through an astrological lens invites a deeper understanding of the impact of Hellenistic astrology on later practices, including those that emerged in the Roman era. The astrological principles established during the Hellenistic period influenced how subsequent generations would interpret celestial events. The involvement of astrology in medicine and healing during this time also provides a backdrop for understanding how the associations between celestial movements and human affairs were perceived. By exploring the astrological dimensions of May 5, 1789, we can appreciate the enduring legacy of Hellenistic astrology and its relevance to the unfolding of historical narratives.

Chart Highlights:

Chart Highlights serve as a vital lens through which astrologers can analyze the pivotal contributions and contexts of key historical figures in Hellenistic astrology. This section emphasizes the significance of whole sign houses and the tropical zodiac as foundational elements in astrological practice during the Hellenistic period. By highlighting how these techniques were employed, astrologers can gain insights into the interpretive frameworks used by ancient practitioners, allowing for a deeper understanding of how these methods continue to influence modern astrology.

The influence of the Hellenistic period on astrology practices cannot be overstated. This era marked a transformative phase where ideas from various cultures converged, resulting in the synthesis of astrological knowledge that would shape future practices. By charting the evolution of astrological methods, we can identify key shifts in thought and technique, illustrating how Hellenistic astrologers blended local traditions with imported ideas, ultimately creating a rich tapestry of astrological wisdom that persists today.

Key historical figures in Hellenistic astrology made substantial contributions that resonate through the ages. Figures such as Ptolemy and Vettius Valens provided foundational texts that not only codified astrological practices but also introduced innovative concepts that expanded the discipline. The chart highlights the specific techniques and philosophies espoused by these figures, allowing contemporary astrologers to appreciate their lasting impact and the context in which they operated. Understanding their contributions aids in recognizing the lineage of astrological thought and its development over time. Astrology played a crucial role in ancient Greek political decisions, serving as a tool for leaders to gauge auspicious times for actions and policies. By examining historical records and astrological charts from significant political events, astrologers can uncover how celestial observations influenced governance. This exploration reveals the intertwined nature of astrology and politics in the Hellenistic world, illustrating how leaders relied on astrological guidance to navigate the complexities of statecraft, which, in turn, shaped the course of history.

The impact of Hellenistic astrology on Roman practices marks another critical area of exploration. As the Romans absorbed Hellenistic knowledge, they adapted and expanded upon it, leading to the development of a distinct astrological tradition that would dominate Western astrology for centuries. By analyzing the transitions in astrological thought during this period, astrologers can appreciate how these ancient practices laid the groundwork for modern interpretations. The chart highlights the continuity and adaptation of astrological principles, ensuring that the legacy of Hellenistic astrology remains a vital part of the astrological dialogue today.

10. Hiroshima Atomic Bombing

Date and Time: August 6, 1945, at 8:15 a.m. (Hiroshima, Japan)

The date and time of August 6, 1945, at 8:15 a.m. in Hiroshima, Japan, marks a significant point in history that resonates deeply within the realms of astrology and its practice. The moment the atomic bomb was dropped, the astrological chart for Hiroshima captured a unique celestial alignment that astrologers can analyze to understand the broader implications of such a catastrophic event. The positioning of planets at this time reveals insights into the collective emotions, political motivations, and the philosophical underpinnings that influenced human actions leading up to this pivotal moment in history. Astrologically, the chart for Hiroshima on that day shows the Moon in a prominent position, reflecting the emotional and societal undercurrents present in Japan at the time. The Moon's placement can be interpreted as indicative of the populace's feelings—fear, uncertainty, and a longing for peace amidst the chaos of war. Additionally, the conjunction of Mars and Uranus in the sky symbolizes the explosive energy and suddenness of the event. This alignment not only signifies the violent nature of the bombing but also serves as a cautionary tale about the unforeseen consequences of technological advancements and military power.

Furthermore, the event of Hiroshima can be contextualized within the broader narrative of Hellenistic astrology and its evolution into modern practices. The influence of Hellenistic principles is evident in the way astrologers can apply whole sign houses and the tropical zodiac to interpret contemporary events. The astrological techniques developed during the Hellenistic period laid the groundwork for understanding the interplay between celestial movements and earthly occurrences. By studying the Hiroshima chart through the lens of Hellenistic astrology, practitioners can glean insights into how past methodologies inform current astrological analyses, particularly in times of global crisis.

The political ramifications of the bombing are also significant, as astrology played a role in shaping decisions throughout history. Historical figures in Hellenistic astrology often used celestial interpretations to guide political choices and military strategies. The decision to drop the atomic bomb involved complex considerations of power, diplomacy, and ethical dilemmas, reminiscent of the methods employed by ancient leaders who consulted astrologers to navigate their political landscapes. Analyzing the Hiroshima chart allows astrologers to reflect on the recurring themes of power and morality, echoing the philosophical debates of the Hellenistic era.

In conclusion, the astrological implications of August 6, 1945, serve as a profound reminder of the intertwined nature of astrology, history, and human experience. The events surrounding Hiroshima illustrate the potency of astrological insights in understanding not only individual and collective actions but also the larger philosophical questions that arise during times of upheaval. By examining this date through the framework of Hellenistic astrology, contemporary astrologers can appreciate the enduring relevance of astrological practices and their ability to provide clarity in the face of historical challenges.

Chart Highlights:

The Hellenistic period marked a significant evolution in astrological practices, with the introduction of Whole Sign Houses and the Tropical Zodiac. This system streamlined the interpretation of charts by aligning each house with an entire sign, eliminating the complexities of measuring house cusps. Such a framework allowed astrologers to focus on the intrinsic qualities of signs rather than the often convoluted calculations previously employed. The adoption of the Tropical Zodiac, which aligns the zodiac signs with the seasons, further emphasized the connection between celestial movements and earthly phenomena, reflecting the Hellenistic emphasis on harmony between the cosmos and human affairs.

Key historical figures such as Ptolemy and Vettius Valens played pivotal roles in shaping Hellenistic astrology. Ptolemy's "Tetrabiblos" synthesized earlier astrological knowledge and established a comprehensive framework that integrated astronomical observations with astrological interpretations. Valens, on the other hand, contributed significantly through his practical approach, emphasizing the importance of empirical data gathered from individual charts. Their works not only influenced contemporary practices but also laid the groundwork for future generations of astrologers, ensuring the endurance of Hellenistic astrological principles.

The integration of astrology into the political sphere during the Hellenistic period cannot be overstated. Astrologers were often consulted by rulers and statesmen, whose decisions were frequently influenced by celestial alignments. The belief that the stars could provide guidance on matters of state, war, and governance led to the establishment of astrologers as key advisors in political settings. This relationship between astrology and politics highlights the pervasive influence of astrological thought in shaping historical events and decisions, reflecting a society that acknowledged the interconnectedness of the cosmos and human affairs.

Hellenistic astrology's impact extended into Roman practices, as the Romans adopted and adapted various elements from Greek traditions. The Romans integrated astrology into their own cultural framework, leading to a rich syncretism that influenced both personal and state-level decision-making. The Roman appropriation of Hellenistic astrological texts and methods facilitated the spread of astrology throughout the empire, resulting in a lasting legacy that would inform astrological practice for centuries. This transition also illustrated the adaptability of astrological systems to different cultural contexts, enhancing their relevance across diverse societies.

Moreover, astrology played a crucial role in ancient Greek medicine and healing practices. Physicians often consulted astrological charts to determine the most auspicious times for treatments or surgeries, believing that celestial influences could affect a person's health and well-being. Texts such as Hippocrates' works reflected an understanding of the interplay between astrology and medicine, with physicians employing astrological insights to guide their practices. This fusion of astrology and healing not only underscores the holistic approach of Hellenistic thought but also highlights the significance of astrological knowledge in addressing human conditions within the broader context of health and wellness in ancient Greece.

11. Discovery of America by Columbus

Date and Time: October 12, 1492, at dawn (Bahamas region)

On October 12, 1492, at dawn, the Bahamas region witnessed a pivotal moment in history, marked by Christopher Columbus's landing. This event, while primarily recognized for its geographical implications, also offers a rich tapestry for astrological analysis rooted in Hellenistic practices. Astrologers examining this date can utilize the concept of whole sign houses within the tropical zodiac to interpret the celestial configurations that would have influenced Columbus and his crew. The positioning of planets and luminaries at this moment can reveal insights into the motivations, challenges, and potential outcomes of their journey, as well as the broader implications for the era. Columbus's voyage was not merely an exploratory endeavor but a politically charged mission sponsored by the Spanish crown. The astrological context of October 12, 1492, provides a unique lens through which to understand the interplay of astrology and politics in the Hellenistic tradition. During this period, astrology served as a crucial advisor in political decisions, with rulers and leaders often seeking astrological counsel before embarking on significant ventures. The configuration of the heavens at dawn may have resonated with themes of ambition, exploration, and the quest for new territories, reflecting the aspirations of both Columbus and the Spanish monarchy.

The influence of the Hellenistic period on astrology practices is evident in the methodologies employed by Columbus and his contemporaries. The techniques of planetary rulerships, aspects, and the timing of events— principles established during the Hellenistic era—were likely integral to Columbus's navigation and decision-making. Astrologers can trace how these practices evolved over time and how they informed the decisions that led to the Age of Exploration. The astrological framework of the time would have provided Columbus with a sense of timing and purpose as he set sail into the unknown.

Astrology's role in ancient Greek medicine and healing also intersects with the historical context of Columbus's voyage. The understanding of celestial influences on human affairs extended to the health and well-being of individuals and communities. As Columbus and his crew faced the perils of uncharted waters, their reliance on astrological guidance may have extended to considerations of health, both physical and psychological. The alignment of planets could have been interpreted as auspicious or ominous, affecting the crew's morale and their capacity to endure the challenges ahead.

Finally, the relationship between philosophy and astrology in Hellenistic culture underscores the significance of the astrological events surrounding October 12, 1492. Philosophical thought during this period often intertwined with astrological belief systems, suggesting that celestial phenomena were reflections of divine will or cosmic order. Columbus's landing, thus, can be seen not only as a historical event but also as a moment in which the astrological principles of his time informed his understanding of destiny and fate. Astrologers reflecting on this date can draw connections between these philosophies and the broader historical narrative, enriching their understanding of how astrology shaped human experience during the Renaissance and beyond.

Chart Highlights:

The Hellenistic period marked a transformative phase in the development of astrology, characterized by the introduction of new techniques and concepts that would shape its practice for centuries. Among the most significant contributions was the adoption of whole sign houses, which simplified chart interpretation by assigning each sign of the zodiac to a house. This innovative approach eliminated the complexities of unequal houses, making it easier for astrologers to convey insights about a person's life and experiences. The whole sign system gained traction among practitioners, ultimately influencing later astrological traditions, including those in Rome.

The use of the tropical zodiac during the Hellenistic era also played a crucial role in the evolution of astrology. Unlike the sidereal zodiac, which is based on the fixed stars, the tropical zodiac is aligned with the seasons. This shift reflected a growing emphasis on the relationship between celestial phenomena and earthly events, reinforcing the belief that astrological influences were not merely abstract but intimately connected to the natural world. This paradigm established a framework for interpreting astrological charts that would resonate through subsequent generations.

Key historical figures emerged during this period, each contributing unique perspectives and methodologies that enriched the astrological discourse. Figures such as Ptolemy, with his seminal work "Tetrabiblos," synthesized earlier knowledge and provided a comprehensive systematization of astrological principles. His emphasis on the importance of planetary aspects and the role of the individual chart paved the way for future practices. Similarly, Vettius Valens, another prominent astrologer, brought a more practical approach to astrology, focusing on real-life applications and the personal experiences of individuals, which helped to democratize the art of astrology.

Astrology's influence extended beyond personal insights, permeating the political landscape of ancient Greece. Leaders and statesmen often turned to astrologers for guidance in decision-making, seeking to align their actions with cosmic rhythms. The belief that celestial events could foreshadow political outcomes shaped governance strategies and military campaigns. This intertwining of astrology and politics underscored the societal importance of astrological wisdom, as rulers sought to legitimize their authority through favorable celestial alignments and sought counsel to navigate critical junctures in history.

The legacy of Hellenistic astrology also had far-reaching implications for Roman practices, as astrological concepts were integrated into Roman culture and governance. The Romans adopted and adapted Hellenistic techniques, embedding astrology into the fabric of their society. Furthermore, the use of astrology in medicine, particularly in diagnosing and treating ailments, exemplified the holistic view of health that characterized Hellenistic thought. By understanding the astrological influences at play, physicians aimed to provide more effective treatments, illustrating the deep interconnections between astrology, medicine, and philosophy in this rich historical period.

12. Martin Luther's 95 Theses Published

Date and Time: October 31, 1517, morning (Wittenberg, Germany)

On the morning of October 31, 1517, the air in Wittenberg, Germany, was thick with anticipation and tension. This date marks a pivotal moment not only in the history of Christianity but also in the broader context of Western astrology. The figure at the center of this shift, Martin Luther, was preparing to post his Ninety-Five Theses, a document that would challenge the Catholic Church and alter the course of Western thought. For astrologers, this event can be viewed through the lens of Hellenistic astrology, which had laid the groundwork for understanding the celestial influences that shape human affairs. The astrological climate on this date provides insights into the potential implications of Luther's actions for both the spiritual and political realms of Europe.

Astrologers of the Hellenistic tradition had long emphasized the importance of timing in human endeavors. The morning sky over Wittenberg was illuminated by a sun positioned in the sign of Scorpio, a placement often associated with transformation, intensity, and deep psychological insights. The presence of Scorpio in the solar chart for this moment suggests a period ripe for profound change and upheaval. This astrological backdrop aligns with Luther's intentions, as his theses aimed to provoke a transformation within the Church and encourage deeper spiritual introspection among the faithful. The connection between celestial movements and earthly events exemplifies the Hellenistic belief that the stars hold sway over human affairs, a concept that continues to resonate with practitioners of astrology today.

The influence of Hellenistic astrology can also be seen in how political decisions were shaped by celestial readings during this period. The Reformation represented a challenge not only to religious authority but also to the political structures that were intertwined with the Church. Astrologers of the time would have recognized that the tensions surrounding Luther's actions were reflected in the broader astrological patterns. The opposition of planets and the angular relationships between celestial bodies could have been interpreted as a sign of conflict and dissent, foreshadowing the tumultuous events that would follow. This intersection of astrology and politics underscores how astrological principles were employed to navigate the complexities of human society.

Moreover, the morning of October 31, 1517, serves as a reminder of the enduring legacy of Hellenistic astrological practices in shaping the medical and philosophical landscape of Europe. The belief that celestial influences could affect health and well-being was a common thread in Hellenistic thought, and Luther's challenge to the Church also prompted a reevaluation of the philosophical underpinnings of authority and knowledge. As scholars began to question established doctrines, the foundations of astrology were similarly scrutinized. This intellectual ferment was conducive to a reassessment of the role of astrology in medicine and healing, as practitioners sought to align their practices with the evolving understanding of the cosmos.

Finally, this moment in Wittenberg is not just a historical footnote but a crucial pivot point that illustrates the dynamic relationship between astrology and the cultural transformations of the time. The Hellenistic astrological tradition had provided tools for interpreting the significance of celestial events, and October 31, 1517, encapsulated the essence of these tools in action. The profound changes initiated by Luther's act of defiance against the Church can be seen as resonating through the astrological framework, highlighting how astrology served as a bridge between the heavens and the earth. In this way, the events of that morning reflect a broader narrative of how astrology, philosophy, and politics were interwoven in the fabric of human experience during the Renaissance, continuing to influence the practices and beliefs of astrologers well into the modern era.

Chart Highlights:

Chart highlights offer a visual representation of the intricate relationships and developments within Hellenistic astrology, illustrating key historical events and figures that shaped its evolution. One of the most significant aspects captured in these charts is the transition from the earlier methods of astrology to the whole sign house system, a technique that gained prominence during the Hellenistic period. This system simplified astrological practice by aligning houses directly with the signs of the zodiac, making it more accessible and practical for astrologers of the time. The charts serve to underscore how this shift influenced not only astrological interpretations but also the broader cultural understanding of celestial events in relation to human affairs.

Another crucial element depicted in the charts is the impact of Hellenistic astrology on political decision-making in ancient Greek city-states. Astrologers often played pivotal roles in advising rulers and governing bodies, using celestial phenomena to guide political strategies and military actions. The highlights reveal specific instances where astrological calculations were utilized to determine auspicious dates for battles or treaties, showcasing the intertwining of astrology with governance. This relationship illustrates how astrology was not merely a personal or spiritual practice but was deeply embedded in the socio-political fabric of Hellenistic society.

The charts also delineate the contributions of key historical figures in Hellenistic astrology, such as Ptolemy and Hipparchus. Their works laid foundational principles that would influence astrological thought for centuries. The highlights emphasize their methodologies, the introduction of the tropical zodiac, and the synthesis of earlier astrological traditions with new insights. By mapping these contributions, astrologers can appreciate the lineage of ideas and techniques that have shaped contemporary practices, illustrating how the past continues to inform the present.

In addition to political and methodological advancements, the charts reflect the role of astrology in ancient Greek medicine and healing practices. Notable texts from the period reveal that physicians often consulted astrological charts to diagnose ailments and determine optimal treatments based on celestial alignments. The highlights present a compelling intersection of astrology and medicine, showcasing how practitioners believed that the positions of celestial bodies could significantly influence health and well-being. This relationship underscores the holistic approach to life and the interconnectedness of various disciplines within Hellenistic culture.

Finally, the relationship between philosophy and astrology during the Hellenistic era is vividly illustrated in the charts, which trace the philosophical underpinnings that informed astrological thought. Influential schools of thought, particularly Stoicism and Neoplatonism, contributed to the understanding of cosmic order and its reflection in human affairs. By highlighting these philosophical contexts, astrologers can better grasp the theoretical frameworks that underlie astrological practices of the time. This exploration not only enriches the understanding of Hellenistic astrology but also invites modern practitioners to reflect on the enduring philosophical dimensions of their craft.

13. Signing of the Magna Carta

Date and Time: June 15, 1215, around noon (Runnymede, England)

On June 15, 1215, around noon, a significant event unfolded at Runnymede, England, which marked a pivotal moment in the history of governance and political thought: the sealing of the Magna Carta. While astrology as a discipline was deeply rooted in earlier Hellenistic traditions, the astrological implications of this historical event provide a rich context for understanding how celestial observations influenced human affairs. The timing of the Magna Carta's signing, precisely at noon, invites examination through the lens of Hellenistic astrological practices, particularly concerning the use of whole sign houses and the tropical zodiac, which were prevalent in earlier astrological systems.

Astrologers of the Hellenistic period emphasized the importance of timing, often associating specific celestial configurations with significant political events. The noon hour traditionally represented the zenith of the sun, symbolizing clarity, authority, and the peak of power. This positioning can be interpreted as a potent moment for the barons and King John, as they sought to establish a legal framework that would limit the king's power and ensure certain rights for the nobility and, by extension, the common people. The astrological chart for this moment could reveal aspects of authority, challenges, and the potential for conflict, reflective of the tensions that led to the document's creation.

The influence of the Hellenistic period on the practices of astrology cannot be overstated. The integration of philosophical thought, particularly from figures like Ptolemy and his contemporaries, shaped the way astrology was applied to political situations. In this case, the signing of the Magna Carta can be viewed as a manifestation of the struggle between the individual and authority, a theme that resonates with the philosophical inquiries of Hellenistic thinkers. The astrological implications of such a document extend beyond its immediate effects, highlighting the way rulers and subjects alike turned to the stars for guidance in navigating their political realities.

Moreover, the impact of Hellenistic astrology on Roman practices laid the groundwork for subsequent astrological applications in Western Europe, particularly in the context of governance and law. The principles established in earlier traditions found their way into the astrological practices of medieval Europe, where astrology was often consulted in matters of statecraft. The Magna Carta, then, serves as a historical touchstone, illustrating how astrological traditions continued to inform political decisions long after the Hellenistic era had concluded. This enduring legacy reveals the profound connection between celestial phenomena and earthly governance.

Finally, the relationship between astrology and medicine during the Hellenistic period underscores the multifaceted role that astrology played in ancient cultures. The principles of astrological timing were not only applied to political decisions but also to healing practices. The signing of the Magna Carta, with its emphasis on rights and justice, can be seen as a precursor to the evolving understanding of health and well-being within society. Astrologers of the past recognized that the alignment of celestial bodies influenced both the collective and individual experiences, emphasizing that moments of historical significance were imbued with astrological meaning, shaping the trajectory of human affairs in profound ways.

Chart Highlights:

The Hellenistic period marked a transformative era in the development of astrology, characterized by the introduction and refinement of several key concepts that shaped its future practice. One of the most significant contributions was the adoption of whole sign houses, a system that simplified astrological calculations by aligning the signs of the zodiac directly with the houses of a chart. This innovation not only streamlined the interpretation process but also allowed astrologers to focus more on the qualitative aspects of planetary influences rather than complex mathematical computations. Charts from this period reveal a systematic approach that emphasized the relationship between the twelve signs and their corresponding houses, laying the groundwork for future astrological practices.

In examining the tropical zodiac's role during the Hellenistic era, it becomes evident that this approach to astrology was deeply intertwined with the seasonal cycles of the Earth. The correspondence between the zodiac signs and the agricultural calendar provided a practical framework for understanding celestial influences on human affairs. Astrological charts from this time often highlight the significance of seasonal changes, indicating that astrologers were not only concerned with celestial positions but also with their implications for political and social events. This alignment of astrology with the natural world reinforced its legitimacy in the eyes of both practitioners and the general populace.

The influence of key historical figures such as Ptolemy, Vettius Valens, and Firmicus Maternus further enriched the astrological landscape of the Hellenistic period. Their writings, characterized by a blend of empirical observation and philosophical inquiry, contributed to a more structured and systematic understanding of astrological practices. Charts analyzed from this era frequently reflect their teachings, showcasing techniques that emphasized the importance of planetary dignity, aspects, and the role of the ascendant. This intellectual rigor not only advanced astrological knowledge but also integrated it into broader philosophical discussions, illustrating the interconnectedness of astrology and Hellenistic thought.

Astrology's role in political decision-making during the Hellenistic period is another critical aspect highlighted in astrological charts. Leaders sought astrological counsel to guide their actions, reflecting a societal belief in the power of celestial bodies to influence earthly events. Charts from significant historical moments, such as the founding of cities or military campaigns, often reveal the timing of these events through astrological analysis. This practice underscored the notion that astrological insights could provide legitimacy to political authority and strategic decisions, reinforcing the significance of astrology within the governance of Hellenistic societies.

The transition of Hellenistic astrology into Roman practices marked a pivotal moment in its historical trajectory. As astrology became increasingly popular in Rome, the charts from this period illustrate a blending of Hellenistic techniques with Roman cultural elements. This synthesis not only preserved the rich traditions of Hellenistic astrology but also adapted them to new contexts, influencing subsequent generations of astrologers. Texts from this time indicate a growing integration of astrology into various fields, including medicine and philosophy, further establishing its relevance in both personal and public life. The legacy of the Hellenistic astrologers, therefore, can be traced through the enduring impact of their methodologies and insights on the astrological practices that followed.

14. First Telephone Call by Alexander Graham Bell

Date and Time: March 10, 1876, at 6 p.m. (Boston, Massachusetts)

On March 10, 1876, at 6 p.m. in Boston, Massachusetts, a significant astrological event unfolded that would resonate through the annals of history. This date marks the moment when Alexander Graham Bell famously made the first successful telephone call to his assistant, Watson, declaring, "Mr. Watson, come here, I want to see you." While this moment is often celebrated as a milestone in communication technology, the astrological implications of such an event can be dissected through the lens of Hellenistic astrology, particularly focusing on the principles of whole sign houses and the tropical zodiac.

In analyzing the astrological chart for this moment, the positions of the planets reveal a complex interplay of influences that can be interpreted through the rich traditions of Hellenistic astrology. The Sun, representing vitality and public recognition, was positioned in Pisces, a sign often associated with creativity and intuition. This placement may suggest that the innovation of the telephone was not merely a technical achievement but also a profound inspiration, linking the realms of thought and communication in ways previously unimagined. The Moon's position and phase during this time further provide insights into the emotional undercurrents of the event, as well as its potential to shape public sentiment.

Moreover, the astrological context of March 10, 1876, can be connected to the broader patterns established during the Hellenistic period, particularly the emphasis on the relationship between celestial movements and earthly events. Astrologers of that era understood the importance of timing in relation to significant endeavors, a principle that Bell seemed to intuitively grasp. The successful transmission of sound through electrical means could be seen as an embodiment of the harmony between the macrocosm and microcosm, a central tenet in the Hellenistic astrological tradition.

The influence of Hellenistic astrologers on the practices of later epochs cannot be understated. As the Roman Empire adopted and adapted these astrological techniques, the significance of planetary alignments in relation to political decisions became apparent. This shift in perspective allowed leaders to use astrological insights to guide their strategies and policies, creating a framework that would eventually permeate various aspects of life, including advancements in science and medicine. The telephone's invention, as a tool for communication, reflects this lineage of thought, demonstrating how astrological awareness could interplay with technological progress.

Lastly, the implications of this historical moment extend beyond mere technological advancement; they touch upon the philosophical relationship between astrology and innovation. The Hellenistic period's philosophical inquiries into the nature of existence and the cosmos laid the groundwork for understanding the interconnectedness of all things. As astrologers reflect on the significance of March 10, 1876, they can appreciate not only the technical achievement of Bell's invention but also the deeper astrological and philosophical currents that shaped the society in which this event occurred. Through this lens, the telephone symbolizes a bridge between the ancient wisdom of Hellenistic astrology and the modern world, inviting further exploration of how these traditions continue to influence contemporary practices.

Chart Highlights:

The Hellenistic period marked a transformative era for astrology, characterized by the integration of various astrological practices and the refinement of techniques that would shape future generations. Key historical figures such as Ptolemy, Vettius Valens, and Firmicus Maternus emerged during this time, each contributing significantly to the framework and methodologies that defined Western astrology. Their works offer profound insights into the application of whole sign houses and the tropical zodiac, illustrating how these systems were employed to interpret celestial phenomena and their influence on human affairs.

The influence of the Hellenistic period on astrology practices is evident in the way astrology became intertwined with various aspects of daily life, including politics, medicine, and philosophy. Political decisions, in particular, were often guided by astrological consultations, as leaders sought to align their strategies with celestial alignments. This reliance on astrology not only reflected the cultural significance of celestial events but also underscored the belief that human actions were intricately connected to the divine order of the universe. Astrology played a crucial role in ancient Greek medicine and healing, as practitioners utilized celestial events to inform diagnoses and treatment plans. Notable texts from this era reveal that physicians often consulted the stars to determine the most auspicious times for medical interventions, reflecting a holistic approach to health that integrated body, mind, and cosmos. This integration of astrology within medical practices highlights a broader cultural understanding of the interconnectedness of all things, a theme prevalent in Hellenistic philosophy.

The relationship between philosophy and astrology during the Hellenistic age was complex and multifaceted. Philosophers such as Plato and Aristotle grappled with the implications of astrological determinism and free will, raising questions about the extent to which celestial influence governed human behavior. This philosophical discourse contributed to the evolution of astrological thought, encouraging astrologers to refine their methods and interpretations in response to the emerging questions of agency and fate. Notable astrological texts from the Hellenistic period not only document the practices of the time but also serve as a testament to the intellectual rigor that characterized this era. Works such as the Tetrabiblos by Ptolemy and the Anthology by Valens provide valuable historical context, showcasing the methods, theories, and cultural significance of astrology in shaping the worldview of the ancient Greeks and Romans. These texts remain foundational for modern astrologers, offering insights into the principles that continue to inform astrological practice today.

15. Sinking of the Titanic

Date and Time: April 15, 1912, at 2:20 a.m. (North Atlantic Ocean)

On April 15, 1912, at 2:20 a.m., the RMS Titanic met its tragic fate in the North Atlantic Ocean, a moment that has since become a significant reference point in both historical and astrological studies. From an astrological perspective, this date and time can be analyzed using the principles of Hellenistic astrology, particularly in the context of whole sign houses and the tropical zodiac. The positioning of celestial bodies at the moment of the sinking provides insights into the broader implications of this disaster, not merely as a maritime tragedy but as a reflection of societal tensions and the hubris that characterized early 20th-century civilization.

In the Hellenistic tradition, astrology was deeply intertwined with the understanding of fate and destiny, particularly in relation to significant events. The chart cast for the Titanic's sinking reveals a prominent configuration of planets that can be interpreted as indicative of calamity and disruption. The placement of malefic planets, particularly Saturn and Mars, suggests themes of loss and challenge, which are critical to understanding the event's astrological significance. Such analyses echo the ancient practices where astrologers would advise leaders and decision-makers, illustrating how astrological insights were valued in guiding public and political actions.

Furthermore, the influence of the Hellenistic period on astrological practices can be traced through the interpretation of events like the Titanic disaster. During this era, astrology evolved as a sophisticated tool for interpreting not just personal destinies but also communal fates. The Titanic, a symbol of human achievement and advancement, was ultimately humbled by the very forces of nature that astrology sought to understand and predict. This duality reflects the philosophical underpinnings of Hellenistic astrology, which posited a cosmos where human actions and celestial movements were interlinked, a theme that resonates with the significance of the Titanic's fate.

Astrology also played a pivotal role in the political decisions of the time, as leaders sought guidance from celestial patterns to navigate challenges. The early 20th century was marked by significant geopolitical shifts, and the Titanic disaster can be seen as a metaphor for the overreaching ambitions of nations on the brink of World War I. Astrologers of the era were tasked with interpreting the implications of astrological events, providing counsel that was often integrated into the decision-making processes of influential figures. Thus, the Titanic's sinking serves as a reminder of the complexities of human aspiration and the unforeseen consequences that can arise when hubris overshadows prudence.

In examining the astrological chart of April 15, 1912, we find a rich tapestry of planetary alignments that not only reflect the immediate tragedy but also resonate with broader themes in Hellenistic astrology. This event underscores the enduring relevance of astrology, as it continues to serve as a lens through which we can analyze historical moments. The contributions of key historical figures in the field have laid the groundwork for understanding how such significant events can be viewed through an astrological framework, allowing for a deeper appreciation of the intricate relationship between celestial phenomena and human experience.

Chart Highlights:

The Hellenistic period marked a significant evolution in astrological practices, particularly through the introduction and refinement of the whole sign house system. This approach, which assigns an entire zodiac sign to a house regardless of the degree of the Ascendant, simplified chart interpretation and made astrology more accessible to practitioners and laypeople alike. The clarity offered by whole sign houses allowed astrologers to focus on the broader implications of planetary placements within signs, enhancing the interpretative framework for both personal and political astrology.

The tropical zodiac, which is anchored to the seasons rather than the fixed stars, became the standard in Hellenistic astrology. This shift was crucial as it aligned astrological practices with the agricultural calendar of the Mediterranean region, thereby linking celestial events with earthly phenomena. The use of the tropical zodiac facilitated a more practical application of astrology in daily life, influencing agricultural decisions and societal events. This alignment underscored the interconnectedness of human affairs and cosmic rhythms, a concept that resonated deeply within Hellenistic culture.

Key historical figures such as Ptolemy and Vettius Valens made substantial contributions during this period, shaping the principles and techniques that would dominate astrological thought. Ptolemy's "Tetrabiblos" is particularly noteworthy as it synthesized earlier astrological traditions and established a systematic approach that combined observational astronomy with astrological theory. His work not only defined the astrological canon of the time but also emphasized the importance of empirical observation in astrological practice, setting a precedent that would influence future generations.

The role of astrology in ancient Greek political decisions cannot be overlooked. Leaders often consulted astrologers to determine auspicious times for military ventures, political alliances, and public events. This practice underscored astrology's integral role in governance, where celestial phenomena were interpreted as omens that could sway the fate of city-states. The reliance on astrological guidance in political matters illustrated the profound belief in the influence of the heavens on earthly affairs, reflecting a culture deeply intertwined with cosmic significance.

The impact of Hellenistic astrology on Roman practices further demonstrates its enduring legacy. As astrology spread throughout the Roman Empire, it was adapted and integrated into Roman cultural frameworks, influencing everything from personal horoscopes to statecraft. The writings of Roman astrologers, who often drew from Hellenistic sources, illustrate a blending of Greek and Roman thought. Notable texts from this period not only preserved Hellenistic techniques but also introduced innovations that expanded the field, ensuring that the astrological traditions of the Hellenistic period would continue to resonate in subsequent eras.

16. Moon Landing by Soviet Luna 2 (First Moon Impact)

Date and Time: September 13, 1959, at 21:02 UTC

On September 13, 1959, at 21:02 UTC, a significant astrological alignment occurred that resonates with the principles established during the Hellenistic period. This date falls within a time marked by a resurgence of interest in Hellenistic astrology, prompting practitioners to revisit and apply ancient techniques such as whole sign houses and the tropical zodiac. Astrologers studying this moment can glean insights into how these systems continue to inform modern interpretations and practices, as well as how historical context shapes astrological meaning.

Astrologers recognize that the influence of Hellenistic astrology extends beyond individual horoscopes; it also played a critical role in societal and political decisions in ancient Greece. On this date in 1959, the planetary configurations included significant aspects that could be interpreted as reflective of global tensions during the Cold War. Understanding these astrological markers allows practitioners to draw parallels with the political climates of the Hellenistic era, where astrology was often consulted in matters of statecraft and governance. This historical lens encourages a richer appreciation of how the ancient tradition informs contemporary political astrology.

Key historical figures from the Hellenistic period, such as Ptolemy and Vettius Valens, laid the groundwork for astrological practices that resonate today. Their texts provide a framework for interpreting the celestial events of September 13, 1959, particularly through the lens of planetary dignities, aspects, and transits. The relevance of these figures becomes evident as modern astrologers analyze how their contributions are reflected in current astrological methodologies and the broader understanding of planetary influences over time.

The impact of Hellenistic astrology on Roman practices can also be illuminated by exploring the significance of this date. The Romans inherited much from Hellenistic traditions and adapted them to fit their cultural context. The astrological events of September 13, 1959, can be seen as a modern echo of ancient traditions, highlighting the continuity of astrological thought as it weaves through history. This connection emphasizes the importance of understanding how ancient practices evolve and retain relevance in different historical epochs.

Lastly, the relationship between astrology and medicine in ancient Greece provides an interesting framework through which to examine the implications of the September 13, 1959, astrological chart. The alignment of planets could be interpreted in the context of health and well-being, a notion deeply rooted in Hellenistic astrology. As practitioners reflect on this date, they may consider how these ancient medical principles can be applied in modern holistic practices, fostering a deeper understanding of astrology's role in healing and personal growth. The ongoing dialogue between historical practices and contemporary applications underlines astrology's enduring significance across various fields.

Chart Highlights:

The Hellenistic period marked a transformative era in the development of astrology, characterized by the integration of earlier Babylonian and Egyptian practices with Greek philosophical thought. The advent of whole sign houses and the adoption of the tropical zodiac represented significant advancements in astrological methodology. Whole sign houses simplified the interpretation of charts, as each sign corresponds directly to a house, enhancing the clarity of planetary influences. This approach facilitated a more intuitive understanding of the astrological chart, allowing practitioners to focus on the relationships between planets and signs without the complexities of more nuanced house divisions.

Key historical figures such as Ptolemy and Vettius Valens played pivotal roles in shaping Hellenistic astrology, contributing foundational texts that would influence future generations of astrologers. Ptolemy's "Tetrabiblos" offered a systematic approach to astrology, merging empirical observation with mathematical calculations. Valens, on the other hand, emphasized the empirical aspects of astrology, providing detailed case studies and practical applications. Their works not only solidified the principles of Hellenistic astrology but also established a standard for astrological practice that endured through subsequent eras, including the Roman period.

Astrology in the Hellenistic world was not merely a speculative endeavor; it held substantive sway over political decisions and public policy. Leaders frequently consulted astrologers to guide their actions, believing that celestial alignments could provide insights into the best times for military campaigns or the appropriateness of political alliances. This intersection of astrology and governance highlights the profound respect held for astrological wisdom in shaping the fate of city-states and empires, reflecting a broader cultural belief in the interconnectedness of human affairs and cosmic events.

The influence of Hellenistic astrology extended beyond Greek borders, significantly impacting Roman practices. As Roman scholars encountered Hellenistic texts, they adapted these ideas to fit their own cultural context, incorporating astrology into their own systems of governance and societal understanding. This cultural exchange not only preserved Hellenistic astrological knowledge but also enriched Roman approaches to astrology, allowing for the development of new techniques and interpretations that would resonate throughout the ages.

Furthermore, astrology played a crucial role in ancient Greek medicine and healing practices. Physicians often employed astrological guidance to determine the most auspicious times for treatments and surgeries. The alignment of the planets was believed to affect the efficacy of medical interventions, with specific planetary positions associated with different ailments. This blend of astrology and medicine underscores the holistic worldview prevalent in Hellenistic culture, where the cosmos was seen as an integral part of every aspect of life, from politics to health, thereby solidifying astrology's place as a vital tool in the pursuit of knowledge and well-being.

17. India Gains Independence

Date and Time: August 15, 1947, at midnight (New Delhi, India)

The date and time of August 15, 1947, at midnight in New Delhi, India, marks a significant moment not only in the context of Indian independence but also for those studying astrology's historical roots and its enduring influence. This juncture represents the culmination of a long struggle against colonial rule, which inherently involves the astrological narratives that shape a nation's identity and destiny. The astrological chart cast for this moment reveals key planetary alignments that offer insights into the collective psyche of a newly liberated nation, resonating with themes of liberation, struggle, and the quest for identity that have been prevalent in astrological discourse since the Hellenistic period.

In Hellenistic astrology, significant historical events are often analyzed through the lens of the planetary positions at the time of their occurrence. The chart for India's midnight independence highlights the positioning of celestial bodies in relation to both the whole sign houses and the tropical zodiac. Notably, the presence of prominent planets in angular houses suggests a time of powerful shifts and transformations. Astrologers can interpret these configurations to understand how the nation's political landscape might evolve in the years to come, paralleling the astrological traditions that have informed political decision-making throughout history.

The influence of the Hellenistic period on contemporary astrology practices is evident in the methods used to analyze the independence chart. The emphasis on specific planetary dignities and the significance of aspects among the planets can be traced back to key figures such as Ptolemy and Vettius Valens, who laid the groundwork for interpreting astrological phenomena. Their methodologies remain relevant to modern astrologers who seek to understand the implications of planetary movements on societal events. The parallels drawn between the ancient practices and the analysis of modern events reflect the continuity of astrological thought across centuries.

Astrology's role in political decisions during the Hellenistic era underscores its importance in shaping leadership and governance. As Indian leaders navigated the complex landscape of independence, they were influenced by the astrological lore that emphasized the timing of actions based on celestial phenomena. The August 15, 1947 chart serves as a reminder of how astrology has historically been utilized to inform decisions that affect the course of nations. The insights derived from such a chart can provide a framework for understanding the challenges and opportunities that arise in the wake of political transformations.

The relationship between astrology and philosophy in Hellenistic culture further enriches the analysis of the 1947 independence chart. Philosophers such as Aristotle and Plato pondered the connections between celestial movements and earthly events, a dialogue that continues to inform modern astrological thought. The philosophical underpinnings of astrology, which posit a correspondence between the macrocosm and microcosm, invite astrologers to explore the deeper implications of the charts they analyze. By examining the astrological context of India's independence, astrologers can engage with historical narratives that inform contemporary practice, ultimately contributing to the broader understanding of astrology's role in human affairs throughout history.

Chart Highlights:

The first chart highlights the profound influence of Hellenistic astrology on the development of astrological practices during the period. Notably, the adoption of whole sign houses marked a significant shift in how astrologers interpreted celestial events. This system simplified the mapping of planetary positions to life events by aligning each house with a corresponding zodiac sign, thus enhancing the precision of readings. The chart also illustrates the transition from earlier methods to this more systematic approach, emphasizing its role in shaping the foundations of Western astrology.

Another chart focuses on the intersection of astrology and political decision-making in ancient Greece. It showcases specific historical events where astrological insights influenced political leaders and their strategies. By detailing instances such as the consultation of astrologers before military campaigns, the chart underscores astrology's role as a tool for governance and its perceived ability to provide guidance in times of uncertainty. This connection highlights not only the practical application of astrology in political contexts but also its social significance during the Hellenistic period.

The impact of key historical figures in Hellenistic astrology is captured in another chart, mapping the contributions of prominent astrologers such as Ptolemy and Firmicus Maternus. Their texts, which synthesized earlier astrological knowledge with new techniques, laid the groundwork for future astrological practices. The chart delineates the evolution of astrological thought, illustrating how these figures shaped the discipline's core principles and methods. Their influence persists, as modern astrologers still reference their works for foundational concepts and techniques.

A further chart examines the relationship between astrology and medicine in ancient Greek society. It highlights the utilization of astrological principles in medical practices, where practitioners would consult celestial alignments to diagnose and treat ailments. This intersection reveals a holistic approach to health that considered the cosmos as integral to individual well-being. By mapping notable texts and practitioners, the chart demonstrates how astrology was interwoven with medical understanding, offering insights into the ancient belief systems that guided healing practices.

Lastly, the chart emphasizing the philosophical underpinnings of Hellenistic astrology illustrates the interplay between astrology and various philosophical schools of thought. It captures how figures such as Plato and Aristotle influenced astrological theories, embedding a sense of metaphysical significance into astrological practices. This chart elucidates the dialogues between astrology and philosophy, showcasing how this relationship informed the ethical and epistemological dimensions of astrology, thereby enriching its cultural context in Hellenistic society.

18. Wall Street Stock Market Crash (Black Tuesday)

Date and Time: October 29, 1929, at opening bell (New York, NY)

On October 29, 1929, the opening bell rang at the New York Stock Exchange, marking the onset of a financial crisis that would be referred to as Black Tuesday. This event was not just a turning point in economic history but also a moment of significant astrological interest. Astrologers observing the planetary alignments and aspects at that moment could relate the tumultuous energy of the time to the principles established during the Hellenistic period. The use of whole sign houses and the tropical zodiac would have provided critical insights into the social and economic dynamics at play, aligning with the ongoing discourse on the implications of celestial movements for terrestrial events.

At the moment of the opening bell, the Sun was in Scorpio, a sign often associated with transformation, power struggles, and hidden dynamics. This placement might have been interpreted as indicative of the underlying tensions within the financial markets, where the façade of prosperity was beginning to crack. The Moon's proximity to the North Node in Cancer suggested a collective emotional undercurrent, highlighting the fears and anxieties of investors. Astrologers familiar with Hellenistic techniques would recognize these astrological markers as reflective of the impending chaos, evoking themes of crisis and rebirth that were central to Scorpio's influence. Moreover, the presence of Mars in Virgo could have been seen as a harbinger of conflict in the realm of commerce and trade. Virgo's association with detail and analysis, paired with Mars' assertive nature, might have indicated a period where meticulous planning was overshadowed by impulsive decisions driven by fear and uncertainty. Astrologers might have looked to the aspects formed by Mars to understand how aggressive actions could lead to harsh repercussions in economic affairs. This analysis would resonate with the Hellenistic perspective that emphasized the interplay between planetary configurations and human behavior, especially in the context of significant societal events.

The historical context of Hellenistic astrology offers a rich tapestry for understanding the role of celestial events in shaping human affairs. In ancient Greece, astrology was not merely a predictive tool but was intertwined with political decisions and even medical practices, reflecting a worldview that saw the heavens as a mirror of earthly conditions. The parallels drawn between ancient astrological practices and modern interpretations during the 1929 crash highlight the enduring legacy of Hellenistic thought. Astrologers today can find value in examining how these principles manifest in contemporary crises, offering a deeper understanding of the cyclical nature of economic and social upheaval.

As astrologers reflect upon the events of October 29, 1929, they are reminded of the lessons embedded in the astrological traditions of the Hellenistic period.

The alignment of planets at that moment serves as a case study in the application of astrological principles to real-world events, emphasizing the relevance of astrology in interpreting historical occurrences. The integration of Hellenistic concepts into modern practice not only enriches astrological discourse but also reaffirms the connection between celestial influences and human experiences, urging practitioners to consider the profound implications of astrology in shaping history.

Chart Highlights:

The examination of historical charts from the Hellenistic period reveals a wealth of information regarding astrological practices and their applications within various societal contexts. One prominent feature is the utilization of Whole Sign Houses, which marked a significant departure from previous methods, allowing astrologers to interpret horoscopes in a more unified manner. This approach simplified the process by assigning an entire sign to a house, leading to more cohesive interpretations. The charts from this era often showcase how practitioners integrated this system into their work, influencing both personal and political decisions in Ancient Greece.

Astrological charts from the Hellenistic period also illustrate the transition to the Tropical Zodiac, which aligned the signs with the seasons rather than the constellations. This shift had profound implications for astrological predictions and the timing of events. By analyzing these charts, one can observe how astrologers began to emphasize seasonal changes as a fundamental aspect of their practice. The relationship between the Tropical Zodiac and its impact on the interpretation of celestial phenomena is critical for understanding the evolution of astrology during this period.

Key historical figures such as Ptolemy and Vettius Valens emerge prominently in the analysis of these charts. Their contributions not only shaped astrological techniques but also provided a framework for the integration of astrology into various fields, including medicine and philosophy. The charts they created serve as essential artifacts that highlight their methodologies and the astrological principles they espoused. This examination reveals how these figures navigated the complexities of their time and influenced the practice of astrology for generations to come.

Additionally, the role of astrology in political decision-making during the Hellenistic period is vividly illustrated through specific charts associated with notable leaders. Astrologers were often consulted to determine auspicious times for key events, such as military campaigns and civic decisions. The alignment of planets and their positions on these charts were interpreted as critical indicators of success or failure. Understanding these historical contexts allows modern astrologers to appreciate the deep-rooted connections between celestial events and human affairs in ancient societies.

The impact of Hellenistic astrology on Roman practices can be traced through comparative analysis of astrological charts from both cultures. Roman astrologers adopted and adapted Hellenistic techniques, reflecting a blend of Greek philosophical thought and their own cultural perspectives. The resultant charts reveal a continuity of astrological traditions, highlighting how the Hellenistic foundation supported the growth and evolution of astrology in the Roman world. As these practices spread, they continued to intertwine with various aspects of life, including medicine, philosophy, and political strategy, shaping the astrological landscape for centuries.

19. First Powered Flight by the Wright Brothers

Date and Time: December 17, 1903, at 10:35 a.m. (Kitty Hawk, North Carolina)

On December 17, 1903, at 10:35 a.m., a significant event unfolded in Kitty Hawk, North Carolina, marking a pivotal moment in human history: the first powered flight by the Wright brothers, Orville and Wilbur Wright. This occasion not only exemplified technological innovation but also resonated with the astrological significance rooted in the Hellenistic traditions. Astrologers often recognize that celestial alignments during historical events can provide insight into their broader impacts and implications. The time and location of this flight offer a unique opportunity to explore the astrological context surrounding the birth of aviation.

Astrologically, the date corresponds with a series of planetary positions that can be analyzed through the lens of Hellenistic astrology, particularly using the whole sign house system and the tropical zodiac. On this day, the Sun was in Sagittarius, a sign associated with exploration and adventure, symbolizing the pioneering spirit of the Wright brothers. Additionally, the presence of Jupiter, the planet of expansion and growth, in the sign of Leo suggests a time ripe for breakthroughs and achievements in human endeavors. The astrological chart drawn for this moment can be interpreted as a harbinger of significant advancements in technology and travel, echoing the philosophical principles of Hellenistic astrology which posit that celestial influences shape human experiences.

The influence of the Hellenistic period on contemporary astrological practices is evident in the way astrologers today interpret such historical events. The foundational texts from this era, such as those by Ptolemy and Firmicus Maternus, provide frameworks for understanding the interplay between celestial events and terrestrial occurrences. The application of these principles to the flight of the Wright brothers allows astrologers to draw parallels between the astrological signatures of innovation and the transformative power of flight. This event not only reflected the culmination of years of experimentation and determination but also served as a testament to the enduring legacy of Hellenistic thought in shaping modern astrological interpretations.

Moreover, the role of astrology in ancient Greek political decisions can also be seen as a parallel to the societal implications of the Wright brothers' achievement. Just as rulers and leaders in Hellenistic times consulted astrologers for guidance in matters of state, the advent of flight opened new avenues for political and military strategies in the 20th century. The ability to traverse distances with speed and efficiency would eventually reshape global dynamics, highlighting the profound impact of innovation on societal structures. This connection underscores the relevance of astrological insights in understanding the trajectory of human progress.

Finally, the impact of Hellenistic astrology on Roman practices can be viewed through the lens of technological advancements such as those initiated by the Wright brothers. The Romans adopted and adapted many elements of Hellenistic astrology, integrating them into their own systems of governance and societal organization. The flight of the Wright brothers can be seen as a modern-day reflection of the pioneering spirit that characterized both Hellenistic and Roman advancements. As astrologers examine the celestial alignments at this momentous occasion, they can appreciate not only the significance of human achievement but also the profound connections between astrology, philosophy, and the evolution of civilization.

Chart Highlights:

The Hellenistic period marked a significant evolution in astrological practices, particularly with the introduction and widespread acceptance of whole sign houses and the tropical zodiac. This transformation allowed astrologers to create clearer and more precise charts, facilitating a deeper understanding of celestial influences on human affairs. Whole sign houses, in which each sign of the zodiac corresponds to a house in the natal chart, simplified the interpretation process and made astrology more accessible to practitioners. The tropical zodiac, aligned with the seasons rather than fixed stars, offered a dynamic framework that resonated with the agricultural society of the time, allowing astrologers to connect astrological events with earthly cycles.

Key historical figures emerged during this era, each contributing unique perspectives and methodologies that enriched the astrological tradition. Figures such as Ptolemy, who synthesized earlier knowledge in his seminal work "Tetrabiblos," played a pivotal role in shaping the theoretical foundations of Hellenistic astrology. His emphasis on empirical observation and the systematic recording of astrological phenomena laid the groundwork for future practitioners. Likewise, Vettius Valens, through his extensive collection "Anthology," showcased the practical applications of astrology in personal and communal contexts, emphasizing the need for astrologers to understand the socio-political dynamics of their time.

The role of astrology in ancient Greek political decisions cannot be overstated. Astrologers were often consulted by rulers and statesmen, as celestial alignments were believed to offer insight into the most auspicious times for action. This relationship between astrology and governance underscores the discipline's perceived authority in informing public policy and military strategies. Notable historical events, such as the founding of cities or the timing of battles, were frequently guided by astrological counsel, illustrating the intertwining of celestial phenomena with human enterprise.

The impact of Hellenistic astrology extended into Roman practices, where it evolved yet retained its foundational principles. Roman astrologers adopted Hellenistic concepts, integrating them into their own cultural and political frameworks. This cross-pollination of ideas facilitated the spread of astrological thought throughout the Roman Empire, influencing notable figures such as Augustus, who utilized astrology to legitimize his reign and make strategic decisions. The legacy of Hellenistic astrology in Rome reflects a continuity of belief in celestial influences on earthly matters, reinforcing astrology's status as a vital tool for navigating the complexities of life. Astrology also found a significant application in ancient Greek medicine and healing practices. The belief that celestial bodies influenced physical health and disease led to the integration of astrological principles into medical diagnoses and treatments. Practitioners would often consult astrological charts to determine the most favorable times for surgical procedures or the administration of remedies. This intersection of astrology and medicine illustrates a holistic approach to health, where the cosmos and the human body were seen as interconnected, further emphasizing the profound impact of Hellenistic thought on various aspects of life, including the philosophical underpinnings that linked astrology with broader cultural and intellectual traditions.

20. First Use of the Internet (ARPANET)

Date and Time: October 29, 1969, at 10:30 p.m. (Los Angeles, California)

On October 29, 1969, at 10:30 p.m. in Los Angeles, California, a significant event unfolded that would resonate through various disciplines, including astrology. This date marked the first successful message sent over the ARPANET, the precursor to the modern internet. For astrologers, this moment serves as an intriguing intersection of technological advancement and the age-old practice of astrology, where the celestial influences can be interpreted in light of contemporary events. The chart cast for this moment reveals a plethora of astrological insights that can be explored within the frameworks of Hellenistic astrology, particularly emphasizing the use of whole sign houses and the tropical zodiac.

Analyzing the astrological chart for this pivotal moment highlights key planetary placements that may offer insights into the cultural and technological shifts occurring at the time. The position of Uranus, often associated with innovation and breakthroughs, takes on a prominent role. In Hellenistic astrology, Uranus was not a recognized planet, yet the influence of its modern equivalent can be examined through the lens of traditional planetary significators such as Mercury and Saturn. Mercury's position in the chart reflects communication, while Saturn's grounding influence indicates the structure necessary for such a revolutionary concept. This combination suggests that the advancements in communication technology were not merely spontaneous but were rooted in a disciplined approach to innovation. The Hellenistic period laid foundational principles for astrology that continue to influence practitioners today. The use of whole sign houses allows for a straightforward interpretation of the planetary influences, offering a clear view of how the energies present at a specific moment align with the themes of progress and connectivity. The significance of the tropical zodiac during this time emphasizes the cyclical nature of human experience, suggesting that the events of 1969 were part of a larger historical narrative where technology and human interaction were evolving in tandem. Astrologers can draw parallels between the cultural shifts of the Hellenistic era and those of the late 20th century, recognizing how the movement of planets reflects societal changes. Furthermore, the role of astrology in ancient Greek political decisions provides context for understanding the implications of this event. The Greeks utilized astrological insights to guide decisions in governance, military endeavors, and civic life. The launch of ARPANET, symbolizing the dawn of a new age of information sharing, echoes the ancient practice where astrology served as a tool for navigating the complexities of human affairs. By examining the astrological climate of October 29, 1969, we can appreciate how similar principles might be applied to today's context, allowing modern astrologers to draw on historical precedents when interpreting contemporary events. Finally, the impact of Hellenistic astrology on Roman practices further underscores the continuity of astrological methodologies across cultures and epochs. The Romans adapted many Hellenistic astrological concepts, integrating them into their own systems of governance and personal guidance. The events of late 1969 can be seen as a rebirth of these ancient traditions, as the world embraced new forms of connectivity and communication reminiscent of the ancient reliance on celestial observation for societal understanding. The chart from this date thus serves not only as a historical artifact but also as a living testament to the enduring relevance of astrology, bridging the past with the present and illuminating the pathways of future exploration in both technology and astrological practice.

Chart Highlights:

The charts within this subchapter serve as a visual synthesis of the complex interrelationships between key historical figures and their astrological practices during the Hellenistic period. Each chart delineates the contributions of pivotal astrologers, such as Ptolemy, Hipparchus, and Vettius Valens, while also illustrating the evolution of astrological techniques, including the adoption of Whole Sign Houses and the use of the Tropical Zodiac. By mapping these developments, we can better understand how these figures shaped the field of astrology and established frameworks that would influence subsequent generations.

One significant chart outlines the chronological timeline of astrological texts produced during the Hellenistic period, emphasizing notable works like the Tetrabiblos and the Anthology. These texts not only encapsulate the theoretical underpinnings of Hellenistic astrology but also reflect the socio-political climate of their time. The interplay between astrology and political decisions is highlighted, showcasing how rulers and statesmen often sought astrological guidance to inform their strategies, thus embedding astrology within the fabric of governance in ancient Greek society.

Furthermore, charts illustrating the geographical spread of Hellenistic astrology into Roman practices reveal the adaptation and transformation of astrological methodologies. This transition underscores the cultural exchange between the two civilizations, where Roman astrologers integrated Greek astrological concepts into their own practices, leading to a unique blend that would dominate the astrological landscape for centuries. The influence of Hellenistic thought on Roman political and social life is crucial, as it demonstrates how these astrological practices were not mere divinatory tools, but essential components of decision-making processes.

In addition to political implications, the charts also depict the role of astrology in ancient Greek medicine and healing practices. By mapping the correlation between astrological signs, planetary positions, and health outcomes, we can discern how practitioners utilized astrology to diagnose and treat ailments. This integration of astrology into medical practices underscores a holistic approach to health prevalent in Hellenistic culture, where the cosmos was viewed as intimately connected to human well-being.

Finally, the relationship between philosophy and astrology is encapsulated in a chart that illustrates the philosophical schools that engaged with astrological concepts. Figures such as Plotinus and Aristotle contributed to the discourse surrounding astrology, raising questions about its legitimacy and efficacy. This philosophical inquiry not only shaped the theoretical foundations of astrology but also influenced its acceptance and application in various fields, from ethics to natural philosophy, thereby solidifying astrology's place in the broader intellectual landscape of the Hellenistic era.

Across the 20 historical events, several recurring astrological themes emerge, revealing broader patterns of transformation, collective change, technological innovation, and shifts in power dynamics. Let's explore the consistent themes and the conclusions we can draw:

Themes Between the 20 Historical Events

Transformation and Rebirth (Pluto and Scorpio Influences)

Many significant historical events, such as the Fall of the Berlin Wall, India's independence, and the Wall Street Crash, prominently reflect strong Pluto or Scorpio placements, which emphasize deep themes of transformation, dramatic endings, and the potential for rebirth. These astrological placements are indicative of periods marked by profound societal change and upheaval, where established norms, structures, or ideologies are systematically dismantled, thereby paving the way for new beginnings and fresh opportunities to emerge in their wake.

Revolution and Breakthrough (Uranus and Aquarius Influences)

Revolutionary moments in history, such as the French Revolution, the signing of the Magna Carta, and the first Moon landing, powerfully showcase the influence of Uranus and Aquarius placements, highlighting themes of innovation, freedom, and significant disruption. Uranus often appears at pivotal moments when humanity boldly takes leaps into uncharted territories, symbolizing groundbreaking breakthroughs that fundamentally redefine the structure of society and the course of human progress.

Collective Identity and Unity (Jupiter and 11th House Focus)

Events that involve a significant collective impact, such as the women's suffrage victory, the historic Apollo 11 Moon landing, and the discovery of America, prominently highlight Jupiter or the 11th House. These celestial configurations emphasize themes of collective values and unity among diverse populations. They reflect the expansion of ideals that resonate deeply across broader groups, often fostering collaboration and a strong sense of unity in the pursuit of a shared vision and common goals, ultimately driving societal progress and transformation.

Authority and Structure (Saturn and Capricorn/Cancer Axes)

Foundational shifts, such as the historic signing of the Declaration of Independence and the significant conclusion of World War II, often prominently feature Saturn or Capricorn/Cancer placements. These placements symbolize authority, responsibility, and the crucial restructuring of power dynamics. This observation underscores the importance of establishing or reforming structural frameworks within society, which can manifest in various ways, including governance, legal reforms, or comprehensive systemic changes designed to adapt to new realities.

Technology and Communication (Mercury and Gemini Influence)

Technological advancements, including groundbreaking milestones like the first-ever telephone call, the historic Moon impact by the Soviet Luna 2 spacecraft, and the pioneering use of ARPANET, all exemplify the themes associated with Mercury and Gemini. These astrological placements indicate that pivotal developments in both communication and technology frequently align with transformative shifts in human connectivity, which effectively serve to break down longstanding geographic and social barriers that have separated people.

Conclusions

Through these consistent and recurring themes, we can clearly observe that astrology serves as a reflection of the underlying forces that drive significant events throughout human history. Each specific planetary placement and sign alignment resonates with the archetypal energies that influence these pivotal events, whether it is through the gradual dissolution of outdated power structures, the earnest pursuit of unity among diverse groups, or the transformative breakthroughs that emerge in the realm of technology. The themes of rebirth, revolutionary change, collective unity, authority, and technological advancement appear to emerge cyclically, responding dynamically to the astrological energies that are present at any given time. This cyclical nature not only highlights the interconnectedness of human experiences but also reinforces the idea that these astrological influences may guide us through the complexities of our collective journey.

Final Insight

The intricate interplay between planetary energies suggests that historical events may indeed follow distinct cycles intricately tied to these celestial movements. Each alignment presents humanity with the opportunity to confront specific challenges or embrace transformative opportunities that arise. By diligently studying these patterns over time, we can gain valuable insights into the types of changes humanity might experience when faced with similar future alignments. This understanding enables us to better anticipate and adapt to the forthcoming cycles of transformation, innovation, and unity that are likely to emerge. In essence, astrology does not predict precise events but rather reveals broader trends and collective archetypes that frequently mirror the significant shifts occurring within the human experience. By recognizing these patterns, we can enhance our awareness and preparedness for the dynamic changes that lie ahead.

Chapter 12: Conclusion and Future Directions in Hellenistic Astrology

Legacy of Hellenistic Astrology

The legacy of Hellenistic astrology is marked by its profound influence on both the theoretical and practical dimensions of astrology as it evolved through subsequent cultures and eras. Originating in the vibrant intellectual climate of the Hellenistic period, this system synthesized Babylonian, Egyptian, and Greek astrological traditions, creating a complex framework that incorporated whole sign houses and the tropical zodiac. These innovations not only provided astrologers with new tools for interpretation but also established a foundation that would be built upon in later astrological practices across the Roman Empire and beyond.

Key historical figures such as Ptolemy, Vettius Valens, and Dorotheus of Sidon played crucial roles in shaping the principles of Hellenistic astrology. Their writings, rich with detailed techniques and philosophical considerations, laid the groundwork for astrological thought. Ptolemy's "Tetrabiblos" became a cornerstone text, influencing both the academic study of astrology and its application in political and personal decision-making. The meticulous methodologies and categorizations found in their works not only enhanced the understanding of celestial phenomena but also fostered a rigorous approach to astrological practice that would resonate through the ages.

The integration of astrology into political decisions during the Hellenistic period further illustrates its significance. Rulers and statesmen turned to astrologers for guidance, believing that celestial configurations could provide insight into the fate of their empires. This practice underscored the perceived interconnectedness of cosmic events and earthly affairs, reinforcing the authority of astrologers and embedding astrology within the fabric of governance. As a result, the astrological charts drawn during this time were not only tools for personal insight but also instruments of statecraft, affecting policies and military strategies.

As Hellenistic astrology transitioned into the Roman context, it underwent adaptations that reflected the cultural and philosophical shifts of the time. Roman astrologers, influenced by the Hellenistic tradition, further developed techniques and interpretations, leading to a rich tapestry of astrological thought that included a focus on individual destiny alongside collective fate. The fervent interest in astrology during the Roman Empire also contributed to the proliferation of astrological texts, ensuring that Hellenistic principles were disseminated widely and incorporated into various aspects of Roman life, including medicine, where astrology informed diagnostic practices and healing rituals.

The relationship between astrology and philosophy during the Hellenistic period established a framework that intertwined metaphysical concepts with practical applications. Philosophers such as Plotinus and Porphyry engaged with astrological ideas, exploring the implications of celestial influence on human existence. This philosophical engagement not only elevated the status of astrology as a field of study but also encouraged a dialogue between scientific inquiry and metaphysical beliefs. The legacy of Hellenistic astrology, therefore, is not merely a historical account of techniques and texts but a multifaceted influence that shaped Western astrological practices, thought, and cultural narratives for centuries to come.

Contemporary Relevance and Applications

Contemporary relevance and applications of Hellenistic astrology can be seen in various aspects of modern astrological practice. The techniques and principles established during the Hellenistic period continue to influence contemporary astrologers, particularly through the use of whole sign houses and the tropical zodiac. These foundational elements have persisted throughout centuries, shaping how practitioners interpret natal charts. The clarity and simplicity offered by whole sign houses allow for a more intuitive understanding of astrological placements, making it accessible for both seasoned astrologers and those new to the field.

The influence of the Hellenistic period extends beyond mere techniques; it fundamentally altered the perception of astrology itself. In contemporary practice, astrologers often draw upon the philosophical underpinnings established by key historical figures such as Ptolemy and Vettius Valens. Their works emphasized the integration of astrology with cosmology and philosophy, imparting a holistic view that is still relevant today. Modern astrologers frequently reference these texts to contextualize current astrological phenomena, demonstrating the enduring nature of Hellenistic contributions to the field.

Astrology's role in ancient Greek political decisions also resonates in contemporary contexts, especially as the world grapples with political uncertainty and social upheaval. Understanding how Hellenistic astrologers advised leaders can offer insights into the potential for astrology to inform modern governance and leadership strategies. Contemporary astrologers can draw parallels between historical applications and modern political climates, using astrological insights to navigate complex sociopolitical landscapes.

The impact of Hellenistic astrology on Roman practices further illustrates its enduring legacy. As Roman astrologers adopted and adapted Hellenistic techniques, they contributed to a rich tradition that informs current astrological practices. The blending of cultural astrological methodologies has resulted in a diverse array of practices today, allowing astrologers to explore various interpretative frameworks and enrich their readings. This cross-pollination of ideas highlights the dynamic nature of astrology as it evolves while remaining rooted in its historical context.

Finally, the use of astrology in ancient Greek medicine and healing practices provides a compelling lens through which modern practitioners can examine the relationship between astrology and wellness. The Hellenistic approach to health and astrology emphasized the interconnectedness of body, mind, and cosmos, a principle that resonates with contemporary holistic health practices. By revisiting these ancient methodologies, modern astrologers can incorporate insights into health and healing, offering clients a comprehensive understanding of their astrological profiles and potential pathways to well-being. This integration of historical wisdom with contemporary applications underscores the relevance of Hellenistic astrology in navigating today's complexities.

Made in the USA
Monee, IL
02 December 2024

71874387R00066